W9-AZW-966

Borrowing God's Glasses

A Girl-to-Girl Look at Life Through His Eyes

By Lacei Grabill

Search for the Truth Publications
3275 Monroe Rd.
Midland, MI 48642
989.837.5546
www.searchforthetruth.net

Copyright 2010 by Lacei Grabill

Borrowing God's Glasses
by Lacei Grabill

Printed in the United States of America
First printing - June 2010

ISBN - 9780971591189
Library of Congress number - 2010924736

All rights reserved soley by the author. The author guarantees all contents are original and do not infringe upon the legal rights of any other person or work. No part of this book may be reproduced in any form without the permission of the author.

Unless otherwise indicated, all Scripture references are from the Holy Bible, New International Version, copyright 1973, 1978, 1984 by the International Bible Society. Used by permission of Zondervan Bible Publishers. Scripture references marked "NLT" are taken from the Holy Bible, New Living Translation, copyright 1996. Used by permission of Tyndale House Publishers. Copyright 1982. Used by permission. All rights reserved. Scripture references marked "MSG" are taken from The Message. Copyright 1993, 1994, 1995, 1996, 2000, 2001, 2002. Used by permission of NavPress Publishing Group.

Published by:
Search for the Truth Publications
www.searchforthetruth.net

Acknowledgments

Thanks to . . .

Keith, my best friend, for his advice and encouragement and for being such an amazing husband and father.

Ethan, Eric, and Kayla for being incredible kids and three of my biggest fans.

Linda Chastain, my mom, for all her support and for being my very first editor.

Marilyn Quigley, my writing professor at Evangel University, for her invaluable advice and revisions to this book.

Jennifer Miller for her friendship, suggestions, and insight.

Bruce and Michael Malone for their expertise in making this book a reality.

Contents

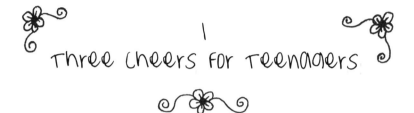

1
Three Cheers for Teenagers

Teenagers are the most awesome people on the face of this planet. If you are a teenager right now, let me just say, "You are amazing!" You are so full of dreams, willing to try new things, ready to take on the world, and hopeful about the future. You see nothing as impossible for you, and you still believe that one person can make a difference. It's during these years that you are discovering who you are, what you believe, and who you want to be. You are beginning to lay the foundation for the direction of your life, yet the concrete isn't quite dry yet. There's still time for some minor or major adjustments here or there, for a change in the building plans, or even for a completely new blueprint to be drawn.

As a teenager, I had more than one of these incidents when I repoured some of the concrete in my life and made some adjustments to my building plans. One major change came when I was 15, and I realized that I didn't like the direction my life was going. I had been going to church ever since I could remember, and I had given my life to Jesus at the ripe old age of 6. I knew all the Bible stories from Sunday school, and I could quote you John 3:16 in 5 seconds flat. But, as I got older, I began to let myself get sidetracked. I wasn't sure if the foundation my parents had started pouring for me was really what I wanted for my life. I still went to church regularly, but, honestly, God wasn't the #1 priority in my life. **MY REAL PRIORITIES WERE TRYING TO FIT IN, HAVE LOTS OF FRIENDS, BE POPULAR, AND ATTRACT ATTENTION FROM GUYS.** Now, if you would have asked me then what my priorities were, I never would have answered with the four I just mentioned. I might have even said that God was my #1 priority because of knowing that was where He should have been. But that was not really the case.

I remember my freshman year in high school as a year of confusion. Since my main priorities centered on pleasing people instead of God, I laughed along with jokes that made me feel slightly uncomfortable, talked about things I had been taught were inappropriate, and would only wear clothes that had the right label on them. I flirted with and dated guys that were far from following God. I ended that year having a lot of friends and feeling like I did "fit in," but I still was not happy with my life.

It was the summer before my sophomore year that I decided to make some changes. I remember wanting to have more direction for my life, a greater purpose for it than what I had before. It was during this time that my youth pastor sent me something in the mail—just a nice "I'm praying for you" card—but under his signature, He had simply written "Jeremiah 29:11." I looked it up, and I found these words:

"'For I know the plans I have for you,' declares the Lord, 'plans to prosper you and not to harm you, plans to give you hope and a future.'"

I'd heard this verse before, but suddenly the light bulb turned on. God already had plans for my life, plans that would make me happier than trying to please people would ever make me. He already had an awesome future laid out for me. All I had to do was trust Him with my life. I've now been trusting Him for the past 16 years, and we've had an awesome time doing life together. Life with Him is never boring, and I've learned to truly believe that His plans are to bless me, not to harm me. I ran across this anonymous poem a couple years ago, and it literally made me cry because I know people who live like this:

First I was dying to finish high school and start college

Then I was dying to finish college and start working

Then I was dying to get married and have children

Then I was dying for my kids to get old enough so that I could get back to my career

Then I was dying to retire

Then I was dying

And I realized that while I was dying to do all these things, I forgot to live.

The writer of this poem missed out on actually living life because he or she did not have a proper view of what life was all about. Sadly, many of us have the same problem. We look at life through the wrong glasses. We think we know who we are, but our lenses are so scratched and smudged that we cannot see ourselves correctly. We believe we know who He is, but in reality, we are quite nearsighted, and we often can't see Him in His entirety. We would say we know who Christians are, but actually our frames are so out of alignment that we sometimes miss out on what it truly means to be a follower of Christ. We have a hard time understanding who we are created to be, yet if we were wearing glasses with the right prescription, we would be able to clearly see His vision for our lives.

My prayer for you is that you will learn how to borrow God's glasses and see things as they really are. If you can learn this as a teenager, you won't forget how to truly live, and you won't get to the end of your life and look back on it with regrets. You will live your life believing Jeremiah 29:11 is actually true. If you can learn to wear His glasses, you will live a life that both you and He will be proud of.

Jeremiah 29:11

"'For I know the plans I have for you,' declares the Lord, 'plans to prosper you and not to harm you, plans to give you hope and a future.'"

Reflection Questions

1. If someone asked you what are the top 3 priorities in your life, what would you say?

2. Does your life reflect your priorities? (All of the time, most of the time, some of the time, none of the time)?

3. Are you happy with the direction your life is going? Why or why not?

4. Have you ever had a time in your life (as I did) when you realized that you needed to draw a new blueprint for the way you were living your life? What happened?

5. Why did the writer of this anonymous poem look back on his or her life with regret? What can we learn from the poet?

Part 1: Who am I?

2 Getting a Clue

I couldn't tell you how many times I've asked myself the "who am I" question throughout my life, but I know that I most often pondered this question during my middle school and high school years. I remember that I could describe myself as the daughter of Danny and Linda, the owner of Sandy (my poodle), and the friend of Jennifer, Melody, and Heidi, but I had trouble getting much deeper than that. I remember the horror of learning the subject of my first sophomore English paper: **"Who I am and where I'm going." I didn't have a clue how to answer either of those questions.** I agonized over that paper, but I'm glad I had to write it. It forced me to do some deep thinking about who I was as a person, what I truly believed in, the things in life that I thought were important, and what I'd like my future to look like.

You see, everyone has a two-part story. The first part is your history—everything that has already happened to you during your lifetime. It includes all the significant events that have made you into the person you are today. For you as a follower of Christ, one of those significant events should be your decision to give Him your life. Some of you, like myself, may have been too young when you made that decision to remember it now. So, the decision I made as a teenager to stop living for God half-heartedly and truly follow Him was a more significant event. Other major events might be a memorable trip, the death of a loved one, an amazingly close encounter with the power of God, the divorce of your parents, the start or loss of a friendship, or moving to a new place. All of these events are part of your history and have molded your character, personality, and outlook on life. They have shaped you into who you are.

The second part of your story (the "where you are going" part) is a conglomeration of all your hopes, dreams, and plans for your future. It's where you want to see yourself in one year, five years, ten years. It's the part that hasn't yet been written, at least not by you. Right now, this is the part of your story that may seem a little frustrating, especially if you are in high school. It's a lot of pressure to decide exactly where you are going with your life. The truth is that you don't need to know all the specifics of that decision immediately. Continue to dream and think about where you'd like your life to go, but don't stress about planning each detail of your life right now. It's already been planned for you anyway. In Psalms 139:13-16 David writes,

> "For you created my inmost being; you knit me together in my mother's womb. I praise you

> because I am fearfully and wonderfully made; your works are wonderful, I know that full well. My frame was not hidden from You when I was made in the secret place. When I was woven together in the depths of the earth, Your eyes saw my unformed body. All the days ordained for me were written in your book before one of them came to be."

Not only did God form your body, he created you with a unique purpose and plan for each of your lives. Although the second part of your story hasn't been written by you, it has already been written by Him. And to top that off, you have been wonderfully made! God doesn't make mistakes or do things half-heartedly. **You are the person you are for a divine reason, made specifically for a divine plan.**

But who is that person? Who are you, and where are you going? Since these questions can seem overwhelming, I am going to guide you with a series of statements and questions designed to help you begin to answer these big questions about who you are. Don't just gloss over this; give it some thought!

Psalms 139:14

"I praise you because I am fearfully and wonderfully made; your works are wonderful, I know that full well."

Reflection Questions

My name is ___Leah___ and I enjoy . . . (What do you really enjoy doing?)

The things that are most important to me in my life are . . .

The significant events that have made the biggest impact on me as a person are . . .

It upsets me when . . .

I feel like my purpose in life is to . . .

It makes me really happy when . . .

I would be totally happy with my life if . . .

At the end of my life, I would like to be remembered by . . .

In one year I would like to see myself . . . (What are your goals for this year?)

In five to ten years I would like to see myself . . . (What are your dreams for the next 5–10 years?)

3 New Lenses, Please

Most of you—even if you don't wear glasses—need a new pair of lenses. You might think that doesn't make sense, so let me explain. Although you are trying your best to figure out who you are, you already have one strike against you. You are trying to look at yourself through your own scratched, smudged, dusty lenses. Most of you have an easier time listing your weaknesses than listing your strengths, and some of you even have trouble believing the good things that others say about you. Why? You don't see yourself correctly. You have to learn how to exchange your own faulty lenses for His perfect ones; you have to learn how to borrow God's glasses and see yourself through His eyes.

So let's talk about how God sees you. What does He think about you? First of all, you must understand that He is madly in love with you. Yes, you heard me. The Creator of the

Universe, the one that spoke the oceans into existence, the one that placed all the stars in the sky loves you intensely. In Ephesians 3:17b-19, Paul prays for the people in Ephesus:

> "And I pray that you, being rooted and established in love may have power, together with all the saints to grasp how wide and long and high and deep is the love of Christ, and to know this love that surpasses knowledge—that you may be filled to the measure of all the fullness of God."

That's my prayer for you, too. I want you to not just hear it, but to truly understand and believe how valuable you are to Him. He loved you so much that He made you in His own image (Genesis 1:27). What's that really mean? We, in some way, look like God. We don't know exactly how as far as the specifics of it. Maybe it's in our physical appearance, in our mannerisms, in our personality, or in the way our minds work. Whatever the case, we are a reflection of Him. We are made in the image of a divine King! How cool is that?

But God didn't just create you in His image and then forget about you either. He is your Father, your Dad. In Isaiah 49:15-16, God promises,

> "I'd never forget you—never. Look, I've written your names on the backs of my hands." (MSG)

You are priceless to Him. In Luke 12:7, Jesus says that you are so valuable to God that the hairs on your head are numbered. God has a running total of how many hairs are on your head (even after you blow dry and straighten it)! That's how valuable you are to Him. But even if you have trouble believing what God says about His love for you, actions do speak louder than words. Look at what He did for you. He underwent immense torture and humiliation and allowed Himself to be crucified so that we could have a real, personal, intimate relationship with Him. Think about John 3:16:

> "For God so loved the world that He gave His one and only Son that whoever believes in Him shall not perish but have eternal life."

Some of us have heard that so often that sadly we don't give it much thought anymore, but take some time to let that sink in. As a parent myself, I can't imagine allowing one of my children to die, much less die the type of death that Christ had to suffer. That took some intensely crazy love for you.

So, if you borrow God's glasses and see through His eyes, you should feel really good about who you are. You are highly loved, valued, and important to the one and only God. I'm a very visual person, so let me try to give you one more picture of who you are. **Some teenage girls see themselves as a plain, worthless styrofoam cup.** They feel very useless and ordinary. They don't see their gifts or potential. They often compare themselves to the other girls around them and think things like,

> "Well, I'm not as pretty as ______,
> as good of a student as ______,
> as good of a singer as ______,
> as good at volleyball as ______."

They've even allowed people's negative comments about them to poke holes in their cup, making it difficult to experience God's love for them. When God pours His love in, they don't accept it because they wonder, "How could God love someone like me?" And so, they let His love run out through the holes in the cup.

The thing that these girls don't realize is that they aren't and have never been styrofoam cups. They are actually crystal goblets—beautiful, ornate, and priceless. They are anything but plain and ordinary, and if they are turned to the light (of God himself), they can reflect a myriad of colors that can only cause those around them to stand in awe of their beauty and gifts. That's who you are. You are that unique crystal goblet, handcrafted by God himself to be beautiful, valuable, and to have the potential to reflect Him in ways that will leave those around you simply awestruck. That's who you are through God's eyes, and since God is truth, that means that's who you really are. That's who you were truly meant to be. You just have to learn to believe it.

Ephesians 3:17b-18

"And I pray that you, being rooted and established in love, may have the power, together with all the saints, to grasp how wide and long and high and deep is the love of Christ . . ."

Reflection Questions

1. Do you have trouble loving yourself? If so, why do you think you do?

2. If a girl doesn't get her value from God, where might she get her value?

3. How could seeing yourself through God's eyes affect your relationships with friends? With the opposite sex?

4. Could getting your value from the wrong place affect how you dress? How?

5. How could you help someone who has trouble seeing herself/himself as valuable?

6. Do you more often see yourself as a styrofoam cup or as a crystal goblet?

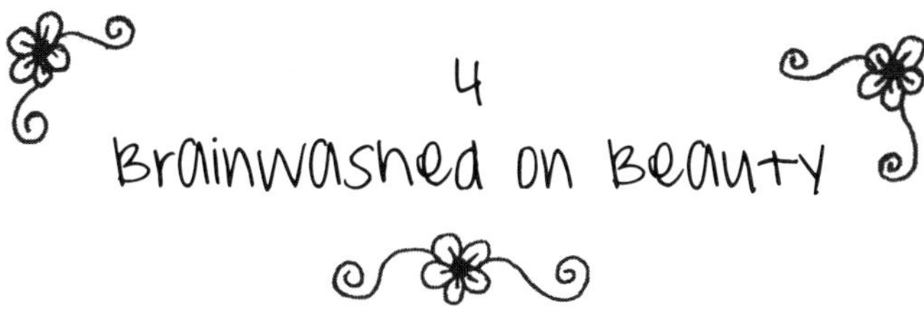

4
Brainwashed on Beauty

If we are so loved and valued by God, why then do so many of us have trouble truly loving ourselves? Many obstacles stand in our way. We must currently live in an imperfect world that, unfortunately, has impacted our way of thinking. In fact, one of the reasons that some of you have trouble loving yourself the way you are is that you have been brainwashed when it comes to defining the word "beautiful."

What? You thought that brainwashing only happened at POW camps and in cults? Wrong! Everything you have watched, read, or heard from the time you were born helps form your perception of who you are. And in our society, as you've probably noticed, outward beauty is highly valued. Most of our T.V. commercials and magazine ads feature people who are seemingly flawless. They are blemish-free, and they have flowing hair, snow-white teeth, and the "perfect body." You know the body I'm talking about. It's the Barbie-doll body (which, by the way, I've decided is basically impossible for the average American woman to achieve). But, our society is all about feeding you the lie that you must look a certain way to be beautiful. I've yet to see a Disney princess or prince who isn't outwardly attractive or doesn't have the perfectly proportioned body parts (with the exception of the Beast who turns into the blond-haired, blue-eyed, muscle-bound man at the end of the movie).

Then there are all the magazines displaying the ridiculous headings about "how to lose 10 pounds and get the body that guys want," "how to go from frumpy to sexy in 10 minutes flat," "how to have a complexion like a movie star," "how to get into that bikini and look great for those summer parties." You get the picture. And if that weren't enough, models are plastered throughout the magazines showing us how we ought to look.

After seeing all of these images of these "perfect" bodies and "attractive" famous people all your life, it's natural to be brainwashed into believing that being beautiful means looking like them. And if you don't look like them, you are made to think that there must be something wrong, and so you need to change yourself to look that way. Take a look at this excerpt from Wikipedia about the causes of eating disorders:

> "The media sends a message that 'thin is beautiful' in their choice of fashion models, which many young girls want to emulate. Both society's exposure to media and eating disorders have grown immensely over the past decade.

> Researchers and clinicians are concerned about the relationship between these two phenomena and finding ways to reduce the negative influence thin-ideal media has on women's body perception and susceptibility to eating disorders. The dieting industry makes billions of dollars each year by consumers continually buying products in an effort to be the ideal weight. Hollywood displays an unrealistic standard of beauty that makes the public feel incredibly inadequate and dissatisfied and forces people to strive for an unattainable appearance."[1]

Teenagers are especially vulnerable to this struggle for a different body. Eating disorders are so common in America that 1 or 2 out of every 100 students will struggle with one.[2] Sadly, we are a culture that puts a great deal of emphasis on body image and weight loss. Think of how many millions of people have had some type of surgery to improve their physical appearance—a tuck here, a nose job there, a little extra in certain places, and a little less in others—all in order to be "beautiful" and valued in our culture.

But what does God say about beauty? Check out I Peter 3:3-4:

> "What matters is not your outer appearance—the styling of your hair, the jewelry you wear, the cut of your clothes—but your inner disposition. Cultivate inner beauty, the gentle, gracious kind that God delights in." (MSG)

The truth is that beauty does not come from how flat your stomach is, how clear your complexion is, or how nicely your hair stays in place. True beauty comes from what's inside of you. The most beautiful woman I have ever met never modeled or starred in a soap opera. When I met her, she was in her fifties and working in a drugstore in a small town in Missouri. But she is a woman who has such inner beauty that I strive to look just like her. Why? She has an amazing inner disposition that includes a crazy passion for people. She worked with the youth (even though she sometimes wondered if she was too old to continue), and she was the most loved youth staff I've ever seen. She knew what it meant to love her neighbor as herself and to put others' needs before her own. She seemed to know all the students' birthdays, gave numerous rides to youth service, took many teens out to lunch, dropped meals off for anyone in need, and cried when she talked about students she knew who were making wrong choices.

But she doesn't just have an amazing heart for people. She also has a genuine love for her Savior, Jesus Christ. I know that when she stands in front of His throne, she will get a crown of jewels that shines brighter than most. That's why she is beautiful. She's beautiful on the inside, and that's what really counts.

> "The Lord does not look at the things man looks at. Man looks at the outward appearance, but the Lord looks at the heart." (I Samuel 16:7)

You may be sitting there reading this thinking, "Yeah, I've heard this before, **but guys don't date me for**

THE WAY MY HEART LOOKS and the popular girls at school aren't popular for the way they look on the inside." I understand your feelings, and I've felt them too, but believe me, as you get older, you will start to understand just how temporary your outward appearance is. King Solomon even warns us about it in Proverbs 31:30:

> "Charm is deceptive, and beauty is fleeting; but a woman who fears the Lord is to be praised."

Most of us will, at one time or another, gain some weight, start finding white in our hair, notice wrinkles that weren't there before, and discover that gravity really does have an effect on the body. Physical appearance changes as the years go by, and so a person that is beautiful only on the outside will only be that way for only a short time. But a woman who is really beautiful—the way beauty should be defined—is a woman who is beautiful on the inside, and she can be that way for the rest of her life.

Believing that we are beautiful is not an easy task for many of us. To help us with this belief, we need to consistently remind ourselves that we are created in the image of a beautiful God. In Psalms 27:4, David asks one thing of God:

> "that I may dwell in the house of the Lord all the days of my life, to gaze upon the beauty of the Lord and to seek Him in His temple."

So, if God is beautiful, and we are created in His image, how can we not be beautiful? If we are God's creation, His masterpieces, and he doesn't make mistakes, how can we not be beautiful works of art? To see ourselves and our beauty clearly, we first have to accept that the things we've been told by this world aren't always full truth. We have to understand that we've been brainwashed on what it means to be beautiful. Only then can we believe God's truth about us and trade in our scratched lenses for His perfect ones.

1 Samuel 16:7

"The Lord does not look at the things man looks at. Man looks at the outward appearance, but the Lord looks at the heart."

Reflection Questions

1. Do you think that you or some of your friends may [illegible] washed on what it means to be beautiful? Who or what have been telling them lies?

2. How would you define beauty?

3. How does God define beauty?

4. What do you believe about yourself? Do you see yourself as beautiful, as talented, as intelligent, as creative, as a work of art?

5. Does what you believe about yourself line up with what God says about you?

6. If what you believe about yourself does not line up with what God says about you, how can you justify what you are believing?

5 Forgive and Forget

"Whatever. I'm not buying it. There's no way that when God sees me, He sees beauty. And why in the world would he love me? I've messed up too many times. You don't know my past and what I've done." For some of you, I just read your mind. While reading this book, you've had the same thoughts. You just can't believe that God could actually forgive you and accept you as His beautiful daughter. Though it's easy to tell someone else to forgive and forget the times when you've made mistakes, how easy is it for you to really forgive and forget your own past? It's not so simple for most of us. Yet, in order for you to see yourself through God's eyes, you have to learn how to forgive yourself.

For some of you, that is a foreign concept because **YOU'VE BEEN BEATING YOURSELF UP FOR YOUR PAST MISTAKES ALL YOUR LIFE.** You've asked forgiveness from

God, and you might have even asked forgiveness from the others who were involved, but you can't seem to honestly forgive yourself. The problem is that when you can't forgive yourself, you will have trouble even liking yourself, much less believing that God could love you. I've been down this road, and it's not a fun one. The thing about us humans is that we have the capacity to forgive, but we don't have the capacity to forget entirely the things we want to forget. Yes, time does help memories fade some, but most of us can remember our past mistakes, especially the really big ones. The enemy and his demons know this too, and they don't play nice or fair. They like to remind you of your mess-ups because they know that it can hold you back from seeing yourself as you really are.

I remember one particular time when I was in high school, I made a bad choice, and I sincerely asked for forgiveness for it. I felt that freedom from guilt that only God can give. Remember that God wants to forgive you and to help put your mistakes behind you. Check out Psalms 103: 8-13:

> "God is sheer mercy and grace; not easily angered, he's rich in love. He doesn't endlessly nag and scold, nor hold grudges forever. He doesn't treat us as our sins deserve, nor pay us back in full for our wrongs. As high as heaven is over the earth, so strong is his love to those who fear him. And as far as sunrise is from sunset, he has separated us from our sins. As parents feel for their children, God feels for those who fear him." (MSG)

When we sincerely ask for God's forgiveness, He gives it—PERIOD. And He forgets about it.

However, soon after I had asked for forgiveness and felt that awesome feeling of freedom, Satan tried to make me doubt that forgiveness, to make me believe that I was still somehow guilty. He wanted to strip me of the freedom I had found in Christ and make me continue to wallow in a state of guilt and shame for my mistake. Fortunately, I realized what was happening, and I discovered a great way to handle the enemy in times like this. When Satan reminds you of your past, you simply remind him of his future! I'd heard people say that or read it on church signs before, but I must say that it wasn't until I was in the situation that I actually believed that it worked. So what is the enemy's future? According to Revelation 20:10,

> "THE DEVIL, WHO DECEIVED THEM [WILL BE] THROWN INTO THE LAKE OF BURNING SULFUR, WHERE THE BEAST AND THE FALSE PROPHET HAD BEEN THROWN. THEY WILL BE TORMENTED DAY AND NIGHT FOREVER AND EVER."

Sounds like a pretty sweet future for him, huh? The next time Satan tries to throw some of your past mistakes up in your face, you remind him of where he is going to end up.

Then you remind yourself of the truth—God's word. Satan wants you to believe that God will not forgive you, that you stand condemned. That simply isn't true. Psalms 34:22 says,

> "THE LORD REDEEMS HIS SERVANTS; NO ONE WILL BE CONDEMNED WHO TAKES REFUGE IN HIM."

I John 1:9 makes it crystal clear:

> "If we confess our sins, He is faithful and just and will forgive us our sins and purify us from all unrighteousness."

Also, remember that in Romans 8:1, Paul writes,

> "There is now no condemnation for those who are in Christ Jesus."

You do not stand condemned for your actions. When Jesus looks at you, he doesn't see the dirty stains from all your mess-ups. **When He looks at you, He sees His beautiful daughter who, because of His sacrifice, now stands clean and free.** Even Satan knows that God's word is truth, and if you use it, he will have to shut up.

I am deeply saddened by the increasing numbers of teenage girls who feel the need to injure themselves in some way to help ease the pain, guilt, stress, and anger that they feel inside. This action seems to have become far more prevalent in the past 10 years. Before that, I'd never even heard the word "cutter." Now that word comes up often in conversations with students. The reasons these girls choose to hurt themselves is varied and often quite complicated. Sometimes they don't even really understand it. Cutting simply becomes an automatic way of dealing with some type of stress. They choose it as a way to gain control over their lives, as an emotional release, as a cry for help, as a desperate attempt to be noticed, or as a form of self-punishment.

But the real, underlying cause behind cutting is that these girls don't see themselves as they really are—priceless, beautiful, daughters of God who can find freedom from their past and have an amazing future planned by the Creator himself. If you are dealing with cutting, I want you to know that God desperately wants to help you. He wants to ease the pain and give you the peace that you so desperately want and need. Psalms 34:18 says,

> "The Lord is close to the brokenhearted and saves those who are crushed in spirit."

Though you might feel alone, you aren't. There is an all-powerful God right beside you who loves you more than you can conceive. Turn your face away from the hurt and look into His eyes. You won't see judgment or anger. You will see eyes overflowing with tears that He's shed for you each time you have decided to cut. Let Him help you. Tell Him how you're feeling. Then, talk to an adult you can trust who is connected to the One who can help you get better.

Others of you can't seem to forgive your own past and see yourself through His eyes because you've been listening to what people have said about you. Maybe you've been torn down all your life by a parent, a sibling, an uncle, a friend, someone at school. Whoever it was, that person has left you with little belief that anyone could love you, that you are valuable to anyone, or that you are going to amount to much in life. Some of these people may not even realize the effect that their words have had on you. They might actually believe that they are acting in your best interest by helping you realize the "reality of life" and how harsh it is. Some may have even been talked to in the same way when they were younger, and they don't really understand how to communicate differently.

Whatever the reason, you need to try your best to put in your earplugs when they start that kind of talk. If at all possible, get away from the person. If that's not possible, and you see him or her often, now might be the time to say that his or her words have hurt you. Help that person realize the effect those words have had on how you feel about yourself.

But above all, you need to realize that no matter who that person is, if he or she is telling you that you are unlovable or invaluable, that person is wrong. You are God's masterpiece, and you are priceless to Him! I know that seeing yourself correctly after being torn down by others' negative words is not an easy thing to do. It's hard to forget the bad things that have been said about you. Yet, remember that we also have a God who "will never leave us or forsake us" (Joshua 1:5). He heard plenty of insults while He walked this earth. He understands exactly how you feel. He'll be there with you every step of the way.

Regardless of what you've done, you have to learn to forgive yourself for your past mistakes. None of us is perfect, yet God still gives us another chance, and He loves us anyway.

> "But God demonstrates His own love for us in this: While we were still sinners, Christ died for us." (Romans 5:8)

God loves you despite your mess-ups. You can learn to love yourself too. He knew you weren't perfect and that you could never be. Yet, He still loved you so much that He chose to die just for you.

Psalms 103:11-13

"As high as heaven is over the earth, so strong is His love to those who fear Him. And as far as sunrise is from sunset, He has separated us from our sins. As parents feel for their children, God feels for those who fear Him." (MSG)

Reflection Questions

1. Have you ever had trouble forgiving yourself for a past mistake? Why was it difficult?

2. How do you accept forgiveness?

3. How do you know you are forgiven?

4. Have you ever tried to earn God's forgiveness? Do you ever think that if you could just be good enough, God might actually forgive you?

5. Have you ever given in and agreed with Satan when he tries to remind you of past failures? How do you fight against that?

6. If you know people who are purposefully inflicting pain on themselves, what can you do to help them?

7. Have you listened too much to the negative words of certain people in your life? How do you stop listening?

Part 2: Who is God?

6 Talking to the Ceiling

In order to borrow God's glasses and understand how He sees things, we must first know who He is. But before we tackle the massive question of who God is, it is of utmost importance first to solidify your belief in His existence. Have you ever found yourself wondering how you can be sure that God is really there? Maybe you've wondered where He is in those times when you feel so alone. Maybe you've wondered how you can be certain that He actually cares about what happens in your life.

For thousands of years, mankind has wrestled with this issue of His existence and what His existence has to do with us. Some have decided that God simply doesn't exist. Other people have decided that a higher being might be up there somewhere, but no one can really be sure about His existencc. Still others have decided that there is a God, but people can reach Him by following the beliefs of Buddhism, Islam, Hinduism, Judaism, Christianity or whatever works for them. I have decided, and it is my unshakable belief, that the God of the Bible is real and that He cares passionately about what happens to me. I believe that He is the Creator of all things, that He actually died so that we could have a closer relationship with Him. I believe that the only way to Him is through believing that Jesus Christ was who He said He was—the Lord of lords and the King of kings. With every ounce of my being, I know that is the truth. But, I haven't always been that certain about who He is.

As a child, I was taught that God was real, that He cared about me, and that He wanted to be involved in my life. But as I entered my middle school years, **I began to have doubts from time to time about whether He really was up there listening to what I had to say.** I continued going to church, reading my Bible, and praying, but I still struggled with those same questions and doubts about His existence and His concern for me. Sometimes it felt like I was just talking to my bedroom ceiling, and I desperately wanted some proof that He was listening. Even as I read my Bible, at times I questioned whether it was actually all true. Yet, I couldn't understand how all these people at my church (who were so sure about God being real) could be wrong. I was confused, to say the least.

Then, I began to experience something that entirely rocked my teenage world. I started having what is called "complicated migraine headaches." They were unlike the usual migraine because the blood vessels in my head would constrict so much during the headache that it would cut off the oxygen to my brain. Since your brain obviously needs oxygen for your body to function, when these vessels constricted, parts of my body would start going numb. I remember once having a headache and being totally unable to move the left side of my body. My tongue would often go numb too, making it quite difficult to communicate. My vision was also affected, and I would see black spots on everything I looked at. As you can imagine, it really freaked me out. My migraines continued to get worse, and eventually my parents had to take me to a neurologist (a specialist on the nervous system), who told them to rush me to the hospital at the onset of the next migraine headache. He said that my migraines had become so severe that he was concerned I might have a stroke.

I vividly remember the morning I started seeing black spots again, which always meant that a migraine was coming. While Mom and Dad rushed around getting things ready for the hospital, I lay in bed crying, afraid for my life. I begged God for help. It was in that moment of utter desperation that God whispered three simple words that forever erased any doubts I had about His existence. He said, "Lacei, sit up." I hesitated, wondering if I had really heard God, and those three words came again, so strong in my mind that I was sure they had to be from Him. I sat up, and the spots disappeared. To this day, I have never again had a migraine headache. To this day, I have never again doubted if God is real.

For me, my personal experience with the living God gave me what I needed to believe wholeheartedly in His existence. I'm sure many of you have also had experiences with God that have helped increase your faith in Him. Or maybe some of you have come to believe in God's existence by listening to others explain why they believe that God is real. A person's story of faith is powerful. People can debate a lot of things, but they can't argue someone's personal experience with God.

For those of you who haven't yet had an experience that erases your doubts, a variety of other evidence points to just how real He is. Josh McDowell's *Evidence that Demands a Verdict* is a detailed explanation of the historical evidence that shows the Bible to be true. *The Case for Christ* or *The Case for Faith* by Lee Strobel, *More than a Carpenter* by Josh McDowell, and *Mere Christianity* by C.S. Lewis are also excellent books that explain why God is there and why the Bible is Truth. If you still struggle with His existence from time to time, I would strongly suggest checking out these books.

If I weren't already convinced of God's existence, I would be further convinced just from looking at my world. After one observes this universe, the hand of the Creator is obvious. Edwin Conklin said, "The probability of life originating from accident is comparable to the probability of the Unabridged Dictionary resulting from an explosion in a printing factory."[3] Believing in the absence of a Creator involves nearly the same amount of faith as believing in Him. Life did not just happen. The amazing landscapes and sunsets of this world did not just appear by chance. We did not just meander into this world by evolving from primates. There was an artist, and he took His time painting and forming His creation into existence. (For further concrete evidence of a Creator, check out *Censored Science* by Bruce Malone.)

Now if you personally are going through a time of questioning the reality of God from time to time and wondering if He really does care about what happens to you, know that God is not mad at you for your questions. I'm sure most of us have had moments of feeling alone and wondering where God went. The song "Never Alone" by Barlow Girl expresses both the gut level feelings of loneliness and the solution as well:

I waited for you today
But you didn't show
I needed You today
So where did You go?
You told me to call
Said You'd be there
And though I haven't seen You
Are You still there?

I cried out with no reply
And I can't feel You by my side.
So I'll hold tight to what I know
You're here and I'm never alone.

And though I cannot see You
And I can't explain why
Such a deep, deep reassurance
You've placed in my life.
We cannot separate
Cause You're part of me
And though You're invisible
I'll trust the unseen.[4]

No matter how you feel sometimes, God never leaves you alone. Your feelings do not determine what reality is.

Reality is that God is here and He desperately wants to show you how very much He loves you. He even gives specific instructions on how you can find answers to your questions, and ultimately discover the reality of Him. Deuteronomy 4:29 promises,

> "IF . . . YOU SEEK THE LORD YOUR GOD, YOU WILL FIND HIM IF YOU LOOK FOR HIM WITH ALL YOUR HEART AND WITH ALL YOUR SOUL."

James 4:8 tells you,

> "COME NEAR TO GOD, AND HE WILL COME NEAR TO YOU."

Matthew 7:7 says,

> "ASK AND IT WILL BE GIVEN TO YOU, SEEK AND YOU WILL FIND; KNOCK AND THE DOOR WILL BE OPENED TO YOU."

Give your all to getting to know God and who He is. Experiencing Him will never leave you disappointed. Experiencing Him will simply leave you with an unshakable belief that He really is up there. Then, you will understand what C.S. Lewis meant when he said, "I believe in Christianity as I believe that the sun has risen; not only because I see it, but because by it I see everything else."[5]

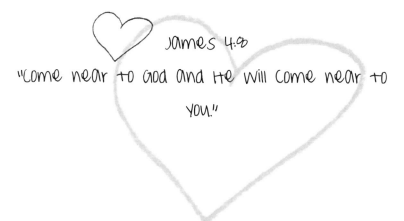

James 4:8

"Come near to God and He will come near to you."

Reflection Questions

1. Have you ever had doubts about God's existence or concern for you? Why do you think you had them?

2. Are you entirely convinced that God is really up there? Why or why not?

3. How do you know that God is real and that he cares about you?

4. What do you think C.S. Lewis meant by the quote that ends this chapter?

5. What does it mean to seek God with all your heart and soul? How do you actually "come near to God?"

7 A Temporary Band-aid

Who is God? What a huge question that is. That question has so many answers that it's hard to find a place to start. The truth is that He is everything, is in everything that is good, and is everywhere. He has always been and will never cease to be. He is all-powerful, all-knowing, and all-awesome (not a word, but should be). So how do I attempt to answer that massive question in one chapter? Honestly, I can't. I can't give you a complete, comprehensive answer to that question even if I sat down and wrote 100 books on it. John admits in John 21:25 that he couldn't completely describe all of Jesus' life:

> "Jesus did many other things as well. If every one of them were written down, I suppose that even the whole world would not have room for the books that would be written."

John is actually saying that God is too huge to be completely described in any number of books written about Him. So how can I answer this massive question about who God is? I only know one way to conquer this feat: I can write about my experience with Him—who God is to ME.

So, who is God to me? He is my Savior. But, what's that really mean? We hear it a lot in church, but I think **WE SOMETIMES FORGET WHAT WE ARE SAVED FROM AND WHY WE EVEN NEED TO BE SAVED.** Ultimately, by my choice to give my life to Jesus and ask Him to forgive me for all the times I've messed up, I was saved from spending eternity in hell (a very real and very awful place). The Bible describes hell as a place of great agony and torment, where there will be "weeping and gnashing of teeth" (Matthew 8:12). I am indescribably glad that I will not spend eternity in a place like that. But, I've learned over time that as awesome as that is, He doesn't just save me from that.

Jesus Christ came to this earth for one reason—to give His life as a sacrifice for our sins. Once again, if you've been in church much, you've likely heard this said numerous times. I'm sure I have likely heard it well over 100 times! Yet, one time when I actually tried to explain that to someone who had little church background, I had a hard time clearly communicating exactly what that meant. Why did we need to be forgiven? Why did Jesus have to die in order for us to be forgiven? Why couldn't things have just continued as they were without Jesus coming to the earth to die? So many difficult questions, and yet the answer to each is vital to understanding why Jesus is truly my Savior.

When God made the earth and all its inhabitants (including us), everything was perfect. I sometimes wonder what life was like back then. Maybe Adam and Eve would wake up from sleeping under the stars, grab a tasty bite to eat off of one of the trees, hang out with God for a while, name some animals, enjoy the amazing scenery God had given them, hang out with God again, and then go back to sleep without a care in the world. What a life! As you probably already know, Adam and Eve didn't realize how good they had it, and they chose to break the one rule God had given them. At that moment, sin entered the perfect world, and God's relationship with mankind was instantly changed. But why? Why was that relationship changed?

To answer that question, you must first understand what sin is and what it can do. **Sin is choosing something else above God. It is doing what is wrong or not doing what is right according to God's standards.** In Genesis, Adam and Eve sinned by choosing to value what the serpent said over what God had said. They decided to break God's standards (which He created specifically to protect them and provide for them). They decided to do things their way instead of God's way. When they made that choice, they chose to be separated from God. Genesis 3:8 makes it clear that Adam and Eve knew that what they did was wrong and felt guilt because of it:

> ". . . THEY HID FROM THE LORD GOD AMONG THE TREES IN THE GARDEN."

No longer were they in right relationship with God. They would now have to experience pain, hardship, and death—all things that they would have never experienced before their choice to sin.

But most devastating of all was that they had to leave God's presence. They had to leave the Garden. Their relationship with God had drastically changed because they chose to sin, and God cannot look upon sin. Isaiah 59:2 says,

> "But your iniquities have separated you from your God; your sins have hidden His face from you."

Since God is entirely holy and pure, a sinful being cannot even come near His presence. This presented a huge problem both for a God who desperately loved His creation and wanted to be involved in their lives and for mankind who desperately needed Him in their lives. A chasm had been created between God and His creation.

But God already had the answer to the problem, an answer which He actually implied in Genesis 3:15 when He explains the consequences of Adam and Eve's choice. He said that the woman's offspring would crush the head of the serpent. Jesus would come to earth born of a woman, and He would defeat Satan. But it wasn't time yet, so He set up a temporary solution for the problem—a kind of band-aid—that is explained in the Old Testament. Before we delve into that topic, one thing you must understand is the idea that because of God's character of complete holiness and righteousness, sin cannot go unpunished. Sin has to be punished, and its punishment is death.

> "For the wages of sin is death." (Romans 6:23)

So, in order to save His creation from having to die when they sinned, God, in His mercy, allowed them to sacrifice animals in place of themselves.

Eventually, it became the job of the priests to offer animal sacrifices for the sins of the people. Then, once a year (on the Day of Atonement), the high priest would go into the tabernacle, into the Holy Place, then through the curtains into the Most Holy Place. This was where the Ark of the Covenant and God's presence abided. If you look at Leviticus 16, you will see that the process the priest went through of preparing himself to go into this place of God's presence was long and detailed. Since God dwelt there, any unholiness could result in death. In Leviticus 16:2, God warns Moses about the power of His presence:

> "'The Lord said to Moses, 'Warn your brother, Aaron, not to enter the Most Holy Place behind the inner curtain whenever he chooses; if he does, he will die. For the Ark's cover—the place of atonement—is there, and I myself am present in the cloud above the atonement cover.'" (NLT)

The high priest would then follow the directions God had given Him for offering animal sacrifices for the sins of the people. But that didn't mean that the people were then entirely forgiven as we are today. Hebrews 10:4 points out,

> ". . . it is impossible for the blood of bulls and goats to take away sins."

An animal sacrifice cannot adequately take the place of a human being who is made in God's image. Consequently, the people still had to follow the Old Testament law—a set of various rules and regulations that were designed to help them stay in right standing with God. Yet, many of them turned away from God and did not follow God's instructions. During those times, God had to speak to the people through specific "preachers" called prophets. Because of the issue of sin, God and His creation were still on opposite sides of the chasm.

Then, God decided that the time had come to do away with the old system—to take the band-aid off and truly heal the problem:

> This new plan I'm making with Israel
> isn't going to be written on paper,
> isn't going to be chiseled in stone;
> This time I'm writing out the plan in them,
> carving it on the lining of their hearts.
> I'll be their God,
> they'll be my people.
> They won't go to school to learn about me,
> or buy a book called God in Five Easy Lessons.
> They'll all get to know me firsthand,
> the little and the big,
> the small and the great.
> They'll get to know me by being
> kindly forgiven, with the slate of
> their sins forever wiped clean.
> (Hebrews 8:10-12, MSG)

Since His beloved creation still struggled with sin which was punishable by death, and because the chasm would never be fixed with the blood of animals, God decided to come to earth and take the punishment that His people deserved. He "sacrificed for their sins once for all when He offered Himself" (Hebrews 7:27). At the moment He died,

Luke 23:46 says that "the curtain of the temple was torn in two." No longer would a high priest have to offer animal sacrifices for the sins of the people. No longer would only a high priest be allowed to go into God's presence. Hebrews 4:16 says,

> "Let us then approach the throne of grace with confidence, so that we may receive mercy and find grace to help us in our time of need."

Jesus' sacrifice allowed us free access to God. It allowed us to not have to be punished by death for our sins.

> "For the wages of sin is death, but the gift of God is eternal life through Jesus Christ our Lord." (Romans 6:23)

Jesus' cross became the bridge over the chasm that separated us from God.

We now have the ability to choose to ask for forgiveness of our sins and become right with our Creator. Check out I John 1:9:

> "If we confess our sins, He is faithful and just and will forgive us our sins and purify us from all unrighteousness."

We now have the amazing privilege of standing before Him pure and forgiven. We now can walk in the garden with God and get to know Him once again. What an awesome gift God has given us! Jesus said,

> "The thief [Satan] comes only to steal and kill and destroy; I have come that they may have life and have it to the full." (John 10:10)

He not only literally saved our lives, but he also gave us the freedom to live. What an incredible Savior.

John 10:10

"The thief comes only to steal and kill and destroy; I have come that they may have life, and have it to the full."

Reflection Questions

1. What does it mean to you to be saved?

2. What is sin?

3. Why did Jesus have to die?

4. How did Jesus' death change the way things were?

5. Why do you need a Savior?

A Green-haired Fan

Who is God to me? He's my Dad. Some people have trouble calling Him that because of the absence of their earthly father. It's hard to totally understand the concept of a "dad" when you've never experienced having one. But God is described as being "a father to the fatherless" (Psalms 68:5). He can provide everything that was lacking in your life. Other people have trouble calling Him by that name because of the failures of their earthly father. When they think of that word "dad," negative images come to mind. Let me assure you that God is not anything like that "dad." He is everything that a dad should be. He is your protector, your provider, and your biggest fan. I was blessed with a great earthly dad who did fulfill these fatherly roles to the best of his ability. But my heavenly Dad can fulfill those roles in ways that my dad here on earth could never manage to do. Let me explain.

From the time you are born, one of the roles of your earthly dad is to be your protector, your bodyguard. Now that job encompasses a great many things. It ranges from keeping you from touching the oven to stopping your older siblings from pushing you down the stairs to meeting your new boyfriend at the door with a shotgun. No matter what the perceived danger, it is your dad's job to get his princess out of harm's way. One way that my earthly dad tried to protect me during my childhood was by installing a security system in our house. Because of my past, he knew that I wouldn't feel safe in the house without it, and so he tried to help ease my fears and keep me from harm. He did his best, but he has limits since he is only human. Let me tell you how my Dad up there, who has no limits whatsoever, fulfills His role as my protector.

Ever since I can remember, I struggled with fear. I remember being terrified of going upstairs alone to put on my pajamas when it was time for bed. I had nightmares often, and I slept with the covers over my head and a row of stuffed animals on each side of my body (to protect me from whatever might come into my room). As I got older, I did ditch the stuffed animals, but I was always afraid that someone was going to try to get into our house. Having our house robbed when I was in 7th grade only heightened that fear, so even as a teenager I was still afraid of being alone. When my parents were gone, I would often walk around my house with my trusty pepper mace can, making sure that I was truly by myself. My fear followed me into adulthood, and I remember lying in bed with my heart racing, quoting Psalms 23 and praying to fall asleep—especially on the nights that my husband had to be gone. I didn't completely understand it then, but I was in bondage to fear. What's that supposed to mean? I was actually being held captive by a spirit of fear, and I could either allow it to stay or I could learn how to fight a spiritual battle.

It was only a few years ago that I started breaking free of this bondage and experiencing true peace. It was a Sunday morning, and the message was on freedom. I remember that the speaker used a pair of handcuffs as an illustration, making the point that God wants to break us free of the things that are holding us back from our potential. I knew I needed to go forward and pray. You know what that feels like, don't you? You get a big lump in your throat, a strange tightness in your chest, and 20 butterflies in your stomach all urging you to do what you know you need to do—to follow the leading of the Holy Spirit. I forced my feet to move and knelt down to pray. It was in that precise moment that I began to understand what Jesus said in John 14:27:

> "Peace I leave with you; my peace I give you. I do not give to you as the world gives. Do not let your hearts be troubled and do not be afraid."

As I asked Him for freedom, I was overwhelmed by His power. He took off the cuffs of fear I had been wearing for so long and replaced them with His perfect peace.

I am extremely excited to say that I have not worn those cuffs again since that day. Yet, even a couple years later, I still have to battle the enemy at times when he tries to convince me to choose to live in fear again. I have to choose to live in freedom. But as I continue to fight and win the battles, each time it gets easier, and I know I've got an awesome Dad up there who is always fulfilling His role as my protector. Romans 8:15 says,

> "You have not received a spirit that makes you fearful slaves. Instead, you received God's Spirit when he adopted you as his own children. Now we call him, 'Abba, Father.'" (NLT)

The word "abba" means "daddy." Because of His Spirit that I've asked to live in me, I am now His child. I am so close to Him that I can cry out "Daddy," and He will be by my side.

Another job of a father is to be your provider. He is to provide you with the things you need for life: shelter, clothes, food, money for shopping, a cell phone, ipod, laptop, and a new car. Okay, so maybe the last five were not necessarily needed for survival, but I know that I used to think I couldn't survive without them! The point is that your dad here can only provide for you to a certain extent. Even if he is the best father in the world, he can meet only some of your needs. Your Dad up there can meet your every need. In Philippians 4:19, Paul writes,

> "And my God will meet all your needs according to his glorious riches in Christ Jesus."

The best part is that He not only can provide for your needs, He wants to provide for your needs.

> "Cast your cares on the Lord and he will sustain you; He will never let the righteous fall." (Psalms 55:22)

So if God can meet our needs and wants to meet our needs, why do so many of us try to handle things on our own?

I've seen student after student not truly see God as their provider. They get so overwhelmed with life—with school, friends, church, sports, band, choir, and work—that they stress themselves out to the point of becoming physically or emotionally drained. Yet, during this time, in the midst of all the chaos, they have ceased spending much time with God because of their busyness. They have neglected to go to God for help in the time when they need it most.

From my own experience as a parent, I think I have some idea of how this makes God feel. One day, my two-year-old daughter was trying to be a "big girl" and get dressed all by herself. She picked out a shirt to wear, and I immediately saw that it was turned inside out. I tried to help her with it, but she quickly grabbed the shirt away from me, letting me know (in no uncertain terms) that she planned on doing this without my help. I sat there for the next few minutes watching her try again and again to get that shirt on right. She tried to put her head in the arm holes, and her arms in the head hole. She even tried to step into it upside down and pull it over her body.

It was so hard for me to sit there, knowing exactly how to help her, and not be allowed to fix the problem. Eventually, she landed in a frustrated, shirtless, red-faced heap in the floor, and admitted, "No me do." As much as she hated to say those words, I was overjoyed to hear them. I quickly scooped her up, turned the shirt inside out, and put it on her worn-out little body. She looked up at me and smiled, as if thinking, "Why didn't I think of that?" and then took off to play without a carc in the world.

As much as I hated to see my daughter struggle with a problem that I could easily help her fix, God is much more heartbroken to watch us struggle in life without asking for His help. Your Dad up there is your Provider. He knows your every need and He wants to meet it. He hates to see you needlessly worried, stressed, frustrated, and in tears over your life. That's not the way your life was meant to be lived. But how many times have you been that frustrated heap in the floor, and yet refused to give all your needs to the only one who can meet them? To my shame, I know I have been there a number of times. My excuses seemed logical at the time, but the underlying problem was I simply didn't think God could help me with everything I was dealing with. I reasoned that I would just have to handle it by myself for a while. I was wrong. You can't handle it without Him. Tell Him your needs.

> "Cast all your anxiety upon Him, because He cares for you." (1 Peter 5:7)

Pour your heart out to Him, and then listen, and give Him a chance to pour into you. Be willing to follow His advice. Your Dad up there can't wait to talk to you about it and provide you with all you need.

Another role of a father is being a great cheerleader, your biggest fan. I remember laughing as we watched the videos my Dad took of my colorguard performances. At some point in almost every show, He would get excited and yell so loud into the camera that we would nearly have to cover our ears. My dad was my avid fan, and he loved to see me succeed in whatever I was doing. My Dad up there is also an avid fan of me—the kind of fan who would paint His face blue, dye His hair green, and write my name on His chest, just to show His enthusiasm and support for me. Is that a hard thing for you to imagine, that God is your biggest fan? I know that there was a time in my life when I had a slightly skewed image of God, and it was easier to think of Him as a sort of policeman than as an avid fan. I thought he went around on His patrol looking for ways I had messed up and reminding me to straighten up or else. Believe me, that's not your heavenly Dad. The truth is that your Dad up there hurts when you fail. Although He is disappointed when you mess up, He doesn't want to pound you for it. He wants to help you get back up and keep going.

I once saw a visa commercial that showed actual footage from the Olympics in which one of the runners injured his leg and fell during a race. In obvious pain, the injured runner began to limp towards the finish line. He was not going to give up his dream to cross that line. His father, who had been cheering him on from the sidelines, couldn't bear to see his son in such agony and ran to his side. The father put his son's arm around his shoulder and helped him across that line. He was his son's biggest fan, and he was going to watch him finish his race. God is the same type of fan. He's got a front row seat in the stands of your life, He's decked out in your colors, and He'll go to great lengths to see you reach the dreams He's placed in you.

> "'I will be your Father, and you will be my sons and daughters,' says the Lord Almighty." (2 Corinthians 6:18)

What an incredible Dad we have! He's always on our side—protecting us, providing for us, and cheering for us in this crazy adventure called life. We are exceedingly blessed.

John 14:27

"Peace I leave with you; my peace I give you. I do not give to you as the world gives. Do not let your hearts be troubled and do not be afraid."

Reflection Questions

1. When you think of God what images come to mind? Is it a right view of Him?

2. What's the "perfect" father to you? What do you want your child's father to be like?

3. Does it feel natural for you to call God "Dad"? Why or why not?

4. What do we sometimes use to help ease our fears and "create peace" instead of turning to God?

5. What happens when you find yourself beginning to feel stressed or overwhelmed? What do you do? What should you do?

6. How does it make you feel to know that God is your biggest fan? Do you find it hard for you to believe?

9
A Warm Towel

Who is God to me? He's my Best Friend. People use that term for anything from dogs to Elmo, but what does it truly mean? What is a best friend? Think of some characteristics of your best friend here on this earth. Among other things, you'd probably say that he or she is always there for you, keeps his or her promises, and gives you good advice. That's exactly the kind of best friend that Jesus is to me. He's the perfect best friend who never tells one of your secrets, misinterprets something that you've texted, or gets moody once a month. So many times I have run to Him when life became too difficult to handle and I felt like I couldn't make it even one more step. We've all had those times when we've felt like we were on a tiny boat in the middle of a raging sea just waiting for the next wave to capsize us. Isaiah 25:4 calls my Best Friend "a shelter from the storm." In Matthew 11:28, Jesus invites us to run to Him:

> "Come to me, all who are weary and burdened, and I will give you rest."

What an amazing Best Friend! I can assure you from my own life that He does follow through with what He says. Let me give you an example of His amazing friendship—of how He is always there when life gets hard, and of how He always keeps His promises.

When I found out I was pregnant with my second child, I was, like most mothers, overcome with joy. But that joy was quickly diminished because I immediately started having complications with the pregnancy. The next few months were a whirlwind of trips to a medical clinic in Porto Novo, Benin (in West Africa) where we were living at the time. After many emergency phone calls to my doctor, continual complications, and total bed rest for months, I couldn't take much more. I was taking close to 20 pills a day, had been admitted to the hospital once, and had already had malaria twice (a serious disease that can affect the unborn baby). I was simply physically and emotionally drained.

It was in the midst of all this that God gave me a promise that I desperately wanted to believe, but found it hard to actually do so in my present situation. He told me that I was going to have a beautiful, healthy baby. Huh? I wondered if He was really up to date on what was going on with my pregnancy. I was continuing to have complications to the point that my doctor thought it would be wise for us to go back home to the United States. She thought it was likely that I would have a pre-term baby. I knew what He had promised, but everything else—medical knowledge and human logic said the opposite. I'm embarrassed to say that sometimes I even tried to talk myself into thinking that maybe I hadn't heard God right—just so I wouldn't get my hopes up.

But God keeps His promises.

> "The Lord is faithful to all His promises and loving toward all He has made." (Psalms 145:13)

I continued to be on bed rest until I was 37 weeks along, and then my healthy, beautiful, full-term baby boy was born at 39 weeks—a true miracle of God and a promise fulfilled. Not only did my Best Friend keep His promise, but He was also with me every step of the way. Even though it seemed like my tiny boat might capsize at any time, He never let the waves engulf me. Even though I felt pretty wet sometimes, He never failed to wrap that warm towel around me and just hold me in His arms, all the while reassuring me that he would never ever leave me or forsake me. My Best Friend is just that way.

Another awesome thing about best friends is that they know you very well. So, they are usually good at giving advice in hard situations and direction for big choices. My Best Friend knows me better than I know myself, and He wants the very best for my life. That's why I always go to Him when I need answers. His word even tells us to go to Him for answers:

> "If any of you lacks wisdom, he should ask God, who gives generously to all without finding fault, and it will be given to him." (James 1:5)

Some students have a hard time understanding this concept because they just don't get it. They don't get how a person can get advice from someone whose voice they can't audibly hear. Ever felt that way? Let me try to explain how this works in my life.

First of all, the Bible is filled with plenty of advice and direction on how to live our lives, and it's written by someone with a whole lot of knowledge about life—the Creator of life itself. Sadly, I've heard students say that they just don't feel like the Bible really speaks to them, that they don't get anything out of it. My first response to them is to ask where they've been reading (to make sure they aren't in the middle of a book that requires a lot of prior knowledge of the historical background). If that's not the case, I ask them if they have been reading the Bible with the right intentions—with a passionate desire to learn from God Himself. You see, God's Word is not meant to be read like you might read a novel you picked up at the library. It's meant to be studied. It's not about how fast you can read it; it's about how much He can show you through it. **It's not about checking it off on your to-do list; it's about gleaning knowledge from God Almighty.** Hebrews 4:12 says,

> "For the word of God is living and active. Sharper than any double-edged sword, it penetrates even to dividing soul and spirit, joints and marrow; it judges the thoughts and attitudes of the heart."

God's word is alive, and there are so many different ways to He can show you things from it!

Sometimes I open my Bible to the place where I've been reading, and the next chapter or verse says exactly what I need to hear. Coincidence? I don't think so! Other times, I don't entirely understand what I've read at first, but after studying it more, I realize what God is trying to show me.

At times, I've even prayed for direction and then randomly opened my Bible to have my eyes instantly fall on a verse that I knew was solely for me. Just tonight I had a question that I was struggling with, and so I asked God about it. I felt like I should turn to a certain book and chapter (because the Holy Spirit placed that thought in my head). I turned there and found part of the answer to my question. God is too cool. He didn't just tell over forty different people to write a book just for fun. The Bible is meant to be "a lamp to [our] feet and a light to [our] path" (Psalms 119:105). It was written to give us advice and direction.

Another way God has given me and my family direction in our lives is through giving us a sense of peace about a situation. I remember when my husband, Keith, and I were praying and seeking direction for what our next step would be as we neared the end of our time in college. We had the opportunity to meet and talk with the pastors of two different churches, and both of them invited us to come to their church as their youth pastor. But, as we prayed about it and talked more with the pastors, we both felt a peace about one of them—a feeling that it was the right next step.

God gave us the guidance and direction we needed when we earnestly prayed for it. It was neither too late, nor too early, but we walked into that church knowing that we were supposed to be there. Since my Best Friend totally knows me, and totally knows who I can be, He gives direction that is always totally right.

Other times in my life, God has simply spoken to me in that still, small voice that is unlike anything I've ever heard before. It's not an audible voice that you can record. But you hear it all the same. It's a thought that couldn't possibly be your own. It's too strong, too random, too not like anything you would have thought by yourself. The times that God has spoken to me like this have sometimes been hard because of this question: "How do I know for sure that it's God and not me?" The one thing that God keeps reminding me of is that His sheep know His voice. John 10:3b-4 describes Jesus as our Shepherd, and us as His flock.

> "He [Jesus] calls his own sheep by name and leads them out. When he has brought out all his own, he goes on ahead of them, and his sheep follow him because they know his voice."

If you are in a right relationship with Him, you have the ability to distinguish between His voice and your own. In my own life, I've learned that ability is increased as you experience that still, small voice again and again. You then begin to have more confidence in yourself to hear what He says to you—and to believe Him at His Word. How cool is it that God uses so many different ways of speaking into your life? Wow, what an amazing desire He has to talk to you.

My Best Friend has and will always be there for me, keep His promises, and give me great advice. He won't let my boat capsize, and He's always there ready to wrap that warm towel around me. That's just the way He is. He can and will do the same for you.

Psalms 145:13

"The Lord is faithful to all His promises and loving towards all He has made.

Reflection Questions

1. Have you ever been disappointed by someone who is supposed to be your best friend? Why is God different? What makes Him different than an earthly best friend?

2. Why is it sometimes difficult to see God as our best friend? Does there need to be a change in the way we view Him?

3. Matthew 11:28 says, "Come to me all you who are weary and burdened and I will give you rest." Think about a time in your life when you were simply in need of rest. Did you go to God for help? What happened?

4. Do you more often read the Bible like a novel or like a book meant to be studied? Are you reading it with the right intentions (with a passionate desire to learn from God Himself)?

5. This entire section of the book has focused on who God is to me. But who is He to you? Look over this list of names for Jesus mentioned in the Bible. (Just so you know, this is not a complete list. There are many, many more!) Circle 5–10 of those that best describe who God is to you.

All in All	Lion of the Tribe of Judah
Great High Priest	Good Shepherd
Good Teacher	Lord Your Redeemer
Bread of Life	Upholder of All Things
Consuming Fire	Love
Counselor	The Way, the Truth, the Life
God of Peace	Morning Star
Creator of All Things	My Wisdom
Hiding Place from the Wind	My Fortress
Deliverer	My Confidence
Everlasting Father	My Helper
I AM	My Keeper
Foundation	My Power
King of Glory	My Rock of Refuge
Fountain of Living Waters	My Shield
Light of the World	My Song
My Lamp	My Strength
Friend Who Sticks Closer than a Brother	Shade from the Heat

Part 3: Who are Christians?

10 Bible Thumpers

You've wiped off your smudged lenses, and you should now see a clearer picture of who you are and who He is. However, to really bring things into focus, you need to have your frames adjusted. You see, without realigning your frames on a normal basis, you can begin to miss things. Your glasses sit slightly crooked, and your vision isn't 20/20. When you put your head down, you find the frames sitting at the end of your nose. The same thing can happen to your understanding of what it means to be a Christian. If you aren't keeping yourself aligned with Him on a normal basis, you will miss out on what it really means to follow Him.

So, who are Christians? What does it mean to be a Christian? I've heard more crazy answers to this question than I care to list. It seems that many people have wrong notions about the word "Christian." To some, they are hypocrites. To others they are uptight, boring Bible thumpers. To still others, they are intolerant, judgmental rule followers. To even others, they are simply people who believe that there's a God. According to a study called The Barna Update, "today only 16 percent of non-Christians ages 16-29 have a good impression of Christianity."[6] In that same age group, 87% said today's Christianity is judgmental, 85% said it's hypocritical, and 78% said it's old-fashioned. Why do so many people have negative perceptions of Christianity? Though the reasons are numerous and varied, I believe it all boils down to a statement made by non-Christians in the study: "Christianity in today's society no longer looks like Jesus."[7]

I've heard people state that the reason they never want to be a Christian is because they feel like "Christians are a bunch of hypocrites." I remember one conversation in particular because I was asked this question: **"Why would I want to proclaim to be a Christian if they act the exact same way as I do? I'd rather sleep in on Sunday mornings."** I understood the reasoning. If being a Christian doesn't change anything, why be one? It seems that here in America, many people have a simple knowledge of who Jesus was. They understand that He was born to Mary, did some miracles, taught some amazing principles, died on a cross, and then came back to life. They may even say that they know that Jesus was the Son of God. Does that knowledge make them a Christian? Let's look at what Jesus says in Matthew 7:21-23:

> "Not everyone who says to me 'Lord, Lord' will enter the kingdom of heaven. Many will say to me on that day, 'Lord, Lord, did we not prophesy in your name, and in your name drive out demons

> and perform many miracles?' Then I will tell them plainly, 'I never knew you. Away from me, you evildoers.'"

Just knowing about God doesn't make you a Christian. It's what you do with that knowledge. **Yet, the word "Christian" has been used to describe people who know about God but don't know God.**

I've also known people who seem to think that a Christian is someone whose goal in life is to tell others that they are sinners and are going to hell. A Christian is not called to try to convict people of their sins; that's the job of the Holy Spirit. Although we are called to proclaim the truth, I Corinthians 13:1-3 makes it clear that we are to do it in love:

> "If I speak with human eloquence and angelic ecstasy but don't love, I'm nothing but the creaking of a rusty gate. If I speak God's Word with power, revealing all His mysteries and making everything plain as day, and if I have faith that says to a mountain, 'Jump,' and it jumps, but I don't love, I'm nothing. If I give everything I own to the poor and even go to the stake to be burned as a martyr, but I don't love, I've gotten nowhere. So, no matter what I say, what I believe, and what I do, I'm bankrupt without love." (MSG)

Proclaiming God's message without love not only gives Christians a bad name, it's also useless. God Himself didn't come to condemn the world, so why do some people think that it's their job to do so? John 3:17 says,

> "For God did not send His Son into the world to condemn the world, but to save the world through Him."

And why did He do this? The verse prior to this one makes it clear:

> "For God so loved the world that He gave His Son that whosoever believes on Him will not perish but have eternal life." (John 3:16)

Leaving God's love out of the message of Salvation simply brings resentment and confusion.

Just a few weeks ago I was talking on the phone with a friend that has been turned off from Christianity because of all the Christians she knew that seemed to be all about the rules. You know the rules I'm talking about. It's the notion that being a Christian is all about following a certain list of dos and don'ts: You don't smoke, drink, cuss, have sex before marriage, or do drugs. You do read your Bible every day, pray before you eat, and go to church on Sundays. Even though Christians do or don't do many of these things, that's really not what following Christ is all about. Just following a set of rules doesn't make you anything.

In Mark 7:5, the Pharisees ask Jesus why His disciples disregard the "rules of the elders" and eat their food with unclean hands. Jesus replies,

> "You hypocrites! Isaiah was right when he prophesied about you, for he wrote, 'These people honor me with their lips, but their hearts are far from me. Their worship is a farce, for they teach man-made ideas as commands from God.' For you ignore God's law and substitute your own tradition." (Mark 7:6-8, NLT)

Although these Pharisees may have been following a set of rules (the rules of the elders), they were just going through the motions. Their hearts weren't in right relationship with God. They were hung up on following a list of dos and don'ts that was not based solely on God's Word. These Pharisees had formed their own rules for what a godly person should and shouldn't do, and then they had acted as if those rules were commands from God. Consequently, they became so wrapped up in their own traditions of what was right and wrong that they had ceased to truly follow Him.

I remember one day during fifth grade recess, I had the awesome opportunity of praying with a girl named Amanda to accept Christ right there on the swings. I knew that she had a pretty rough home life and didn't know much about church or following Christ, so I had made it my mission to tell her about Jesus. I had great intentions. However, after she prayed and the teacher blew the whistle to come back inside, she asked me a question: "So, what do I do now?" I was a little surprised by the question, but, being a good church girl, I knew the answer. I blurted out, "Well, you don't cuss or smoke and you have to go to church and read your Bible." She said, "Oh," and I think that was the last conversation I had with her about her decision that day at recess. I wish I knew what happened to Amanda. I wish I could tell her what I know now. It's not following the rules that makes someone a Christian; it's a matter of the heart.

Other people have the definition of the word "Christian" partly right. They think that a Christian is someone who believes that there is a God. That's true, but that's not all. James 2:14-18 makes it clear that it takes more than just belief in God to be a true follower of Christ:

> "Dear friends, do you think you'll get anywhere in this if you learn all the right words but never do anything? Does merely talking about faith indicate that a person really has it? For instance, you come upon an old friend dressed in rags and half-starved and say, 'Good morning, friend! Be clothed in Christ! Be filled with the Holy Spirit!' and walk off without providing so much as a coat or a cup of soup—where does that get you? Isn't it obvious that God-talk without God-acts is outrageous nonsense? I can already hear one of you agreeing by saying, 'Sounds good. You take care of the faith department, I'll handle the works department.' Not so fast. You can no more show me your works apart from your faith than I can show you my faith apart from my works. Faith and works, works and faith, fit together hand in glove." (MSG)

Then, check out verse 19:

> "You say you have faith, for you believe that there is one God. Good for you! Even the demons believe this, and they tremble in terror." (NLT)

If being a "Christian" means that you believe that there is a God, then Satan would be a Christian. How messed up is that? True Christians back up their faith in Him with action. They not only talk about God, but they also live a life that demonstrates their love for Him.

So if all these are faulty definitions of the word "Christian," then what is a right definition? The word "Christian" actually means "follower of Christ." It was first used by the believers in the church of Antioch to describe the disciples. Put simply, Christians are people who imitate Christ. They are people who have decided do this:

> "put off [their] old self, which is being corrupted by its deceitful desires; to be made new in the attitude of [their] minds; and to put on the new self, created to be like God in true righteousness and holiness." (Ephesians 4:22-24)

They are normal people who have realized that they messed up and that they need a Savior. Yet, they are people who have not just made Him their Savior but have also made Him their Lord. They are people who are literally trying to be Christ in their world. So how do you do that? Do you dress in a robe and sandals and find some water to turn into wine? No, you look at the basic principles in life that He deemed important. Then, you model your life accordingly. What were His priorities? To find out, look with me at Mark 12:28-31:

> "One of the teachers of the law came and heard them debating. Noticing that Jesus had given them a good answer, he asked him, 'Of all the commandments, which is the most important?' 'The most important one,' answered Jesus, 'is this: Hear, O Israel: The Lord our God, the Lord is one. Love the Lord your God with all your heart and with all your soul and with all your mind and with all your strength. The second is this: Love your neighbor as yourself. There is no commandment greater than these.'"

Jesus makes it simple. **The most important commandment in life is to love God and to love people. That's what being a Christian is all about.** Ephesians 5:1 says,

> "Be imitators of God, therefore, as dearly loved children, and live a life of love, just as Christ loved us and gave himself up for us as a fragrant offering and sacrifice to God."

If you are a Christian, you want to imitate Christ. If you want to imitate Christ, you must learn to do two things. Love God, and love people. If you do these two things, Christianity in today's society will begin to look more like Jesus.

Mark 12:30-31

"Love the Lord your God with all your heart and with all your soul and with all your mind and with all your strength. The second is this: Love your neighbor as yourself. There is no commandment greater than these."

Reflection Questions

1. What are/were some of your faulty beliefs about Christianity?

2. Do you know people who have a faulty perception of who Christians are? What has caused them to think that way?

3. One of the best ways to share your faith with someone and overcome the misperceptions of the word "Christian" is to tell your story. You explain why you chose to give your life to Christ, why you choose to serve Him now, and how He has changed you, used you, healed you, blessed you, given you guidance, etc. So, what's your story? Take some time to write it out on a separate sheet of paper.

4. How would you have answered the question that Amanda asked me: "So what do I do now?"

5. Have you ever assumed someone wasn't a Christian, but you were wrong? What made you assume that? Were you substituting your traditions for God's commands? Explain.

6. How can you know if someone is a Christian or not?

7. How can you change the way people view Christians ?

11
Getting Out of the Lawn Chair

Jesus said it: Love God, and love people. But how do you actually do that? Think of the people in your life that you truly love right now. Why do you love them? Maybe it's because of all they've done for you or that they've always been there for you. Maybe you love them for their personality, the way they always encourage you, or the way they laugh at the same things you do. Maybe you love them because of how much they care about you.

Whatever the reasons, in order to truly love someone, there is one thing you have to do first: you have to get to know them. Yes, sometimes you hear the sappy love stories that talk of love at first sight. Let me let you in on a little secret. There's no such thing as love at first sight. Maybe she fell in love with his stunning blue eyes or his rock hard abs at first sight, but she didn't fall in love with him! You have to know a person well before you truly learn to love him or her. The same principle applies with God. If you want to truly learn how to love God, what should you do? You get to know Him!

Some of you may already be thinking, "But I already love God, and I already know Him!" You are probably right. Most of you have already begun your relationship with God and you do love and know Him. But how well do you know Him? How deep is that love? Is it continually growing? Do you love him with all your heart, mind, soul, and strength? After dating my husband for a number of months, I told people (and him) that I loved him, and it was the truth. I did love him. However, now, after dating and being married to him for nearly 15 ½ years, my love for him is far different from what it was after a few months of dating. It is a far deeper love, a more mature love, a more committed love.

Imagine you are at a campfire. You are sitting around eating s'mores, watching the flames, and trying to keep the bugs away. Someone puts another log on the fire, and all of a sudden the flames get higher and the heat is more intense. The wood is now popping, and it's a great time to roast hotdogs. You can even feel the warmth of the fire on your face, and you have to scoot your lawn chair back a couple of feet. But after you get done eating, everyone gets busy talking, and no one wants to put any more wood on the fire. It continues to get smaller and smaller until it eventually dies. All that is left then are smoldering ashes, not very pretty and not much use for anything.

Now think about the campfire in comparison with falling in love with God. We all enjoy those times with God when the flames are high, and the heat is intense. In those times, our love for Him is growing, and He is using us, blessing us, and talking to us in amazing ways. But, there are other times when the fire seems to be dying, when you can hardly feel any heat, when you feel distanced from God. Why is that? Though there may be a variety of reasons for your feelings, it really all comes down to your desire to keep your fire going. A campfire will not continue to burn on its own. **You will continue to grow in your love for Him only as you continue to decide to put wood on the fire.** Learning to love God with all your heart, soul, mind, and strength is a process. To learn how to love Him more, you have to learn how to desire Him more. Let me explain this with some examples of what I've seen happen.

I've seen teenagers decide to follow Christ and have a complete life transformation. They loved God and were willing to change the world for Him. They lit their campfire. But then after months or years, life got hard and somehow that love for God was not as strong as it once was. The fire was beginning to die. But instead of getting off their lawn chair to put another log on the fire, they turned their back on God. They decided to completely go back to the life they were living before their decision to follow Christ with no desire to turn back to Him. Only ashes were left. So what happened? Did they not ever truly love God?

I've also seen the opposite happen. Students gave their lives to Christ and began a process of falling more and more in love with Him. They had a brilliant campfire. I've seen them struggle with issues but find victory and freedom by turning to God and entrusting Him with their lives. In those students, I saw rapid spiritual growth and an intense desire just to be with Him. Their campfire turned into a bonfire—with flames so high that it heated up everyone around them. So what happened? Do they have some special formula for an amazing love relationship with God? Does God just like them more?

The difference in these two groups of students is the desire factor. The first group did truly love God, but that love never grew into mature, committed love. Why? They didn't desire God enough to take the time to continue to fuel their relationship. They didn't take the time to get to know God in a deeper way. So, when the storms of life hit and life got hard, they abandoned their campfire. They left it to die. They had experienced a love for God, but it was not a committed love. The second group also encountered hardships in life (as all of us do), but they realized that the One who calms storms was right beside them. They remembered, even in the busyness of life, that their campfire must have more wood to continue to burn.

Sadly, I've also seen many students between the two groups. **They haven't totally turned their back on God, but they aren't falling more in love with Him either.** They have decided to follow God, and they do love Him. They've never decided to stop following Him, but they've also never put very many logs on the fire. They've put just enough wood on to keep it going. They are content to just remain in an immature, stagnant love relationship with Christ—with a fire that puts out little heat and sometimes looks like it might die. The crazy thing is that many of them seem to be satisfied to be there. I've never understood that. Why settle for a tiny, insignificant campfire when you could have a huge bonfire? The bottom line is that they don't have enough desire to put forth the effort to get to know Him more. They don't have enough desire to get off their behinds and put another log on the fire!

I've often wished there were some way of giving a person a dose of desire for God. It would be so cool if there were a "desire vaccination," and suddenly a student would jump off her backside and go after God. Unfortunately, no such medication exists. I've heard students say that they want to be closer to God, that they want to know Him more, that they want to fall more in love with Him. Often these statements are followed by this word: "but." "I want to get closer to God and spend time with Him **BUT** I'm just so busy with school, **BUT** I've been so tired lately, **BUT** my job's been really stressful, **BUT** I don't want to give up ________, **BUT** life has just been hard. The saddest part of these statements is that what they are really saying is this: "I want to get closer to God, **BUT** I don't want it badly enough right now to actually do something about it."

So how do you manufacture desire for God? How do you make people want to get up off their lawn chairs and put some more wood on their fire? Can you just muster up some desire by shouting, "I want more of God"? Just recently my husband told the story of when he ran a half marathon. During the last part of the race, all he could think about was how thirsty he was, about how much he needed fluids. After he crossed the finish line, the kids and I went over to congratulate him. The kids were so excited to see him, and we were all so proud of him! But, to our surprise, he didn't even smile when he saw us. The only thing he could do was to whisper "Gatorade."

That's what our thirst for God should be like. Unfortunately, I know that my desire for God has at times been more of a casual thirsting. I would feel a little thirsty, so I would take a drink here or there, but there wasn't really an intense longing for Him. My problem was that I wasn't willing to entirely commit to running the whole distance, to giving my all to know God. As said so eloquently by one of our youth staff, in order to get really thirsty, you have to run the race.

So how do you thirst for Him so badly that all you can whisper is "Jesus"? One way is by becoming aware of your own weaknesses. As you truly recognize the areas where you are weak, you will also begin to recognize just how badly you need God to help you. You will become desperate for His help; consequently, your desire for Him will increase. So, make a conscious effort to figure out your weaknesses and find the source of them. This isn't a fun or popular thing to do because most of us would rather push them aside and pretend like they aren't there. We would rather be self-reliant. But relying on yourself will only cause you to be less reliant on Him.

Another way to increase your desire for God is to try to do something that by yourself would be extremely difficult. Accept a task which forces you to rely solely on Him for help, something that makes you get out of your comfort zone and sweat a little. Just recently God taught me a lesson on this one. **FOR A WHILE NOW, I'VE STRUGGLED FROM TIME TO TIME WITH THE THOUGHT THAT I'M NOT VERY GOOD AT PRAYING OUT LOUD,** especially for other people. I've compared myself to other eloquent prayer warriors and felt that I was lacking. I felt as if I stumbled over my words and searched for things to say just to fill in the "allotted time" I was supposed to give each student. I wanted to pray God's heart, but I felt as though I often was just praying mine.

A little while ago, our church had a prayer meeting, and I felt impressed to go pray for the students that had come forward. I hesitated, feeling those doubts again, and God urged me forward telling me that He would give me the words. I walked up to the front totally uncomfortable and desperate for God to meet me in my weakness. Yeah, I could have prayed on my own strength, from my own thoughts, but I knew that these students deserved so much more. So, I stepped out in faith and believed that God would help me. The results were amazing. I heard my own voice, but I knew it was not my words that were coming out of it. God was praying through me, and He did such a better job than I ever did! I realized that I was trying to be self-reliant instead of God-reliant. It's only in being God-reliant that we become desperate for Him, which in turn increases our desire for Him.

In 2 Corinthians 12, Paul writes about a weakness that He had. He calls it a "thorn in his flesh" and he mentions that He had pleaded with God to take it away from him. In verse 9, Paul tells us God's reply:

> "My grace is sufficient for you, for my power is made perfect in your weakness."

By understanding your weaknesses, you become desperate for God's help. By stepping out of your comfort zone and relying solely on Him, you can allow God to move through you to do things that you never could have done on your own. You can develop a hunger and desire for God that you never thought you'd have. You can accomplish things that you never thought you could do. You can build a bonfire so high and so hot that your whole neighborhood can see it, and everyone around you can feel it. But you will never do anything if you just continue to sit around your campfire, talking with friends, eating your s'mores, and wishing that the flames were a little higher. You have to want to put more logs on your fire. You must increase the desire to fall more in love with Him.

The questions "How badly do you want to know God?" and "How much do you really want to fall more in love with Him?" can be answered by only one person—you. You decide if you will sincerely say what Paul said in Philippians 3:7-8:

> "What is more, I consider everything a loss compared to the surpassing greatness of knowing Christ Jesus my Lord, for whose sake I have lost all things. I consider them rubbish, that I may gain Christ."

You decide if you're going to be content with the size of your fire. It's your choice. God doesn't even make the choice for you.

> "Here I am! I stand at the door and knock. If anyone hears my voice and opens the door, I will come in and eat with him and he with me." (Revelation 3:20)

He will wait for you, but you can't afford to make Him wait. A fire that is not given new wood will not stay the same size forever; it will eventually begin to die.

Philippians 3:8

"What is more, I consider everything a loss compared to the surpassing greatness of knowing Christ Jesus my Lord, for whose sake I have lost all things."

Reflection Questions

1. Why do you love God? Take some time to really think about your answer to this question, not what you've heard from others. Name at least 5 reasons you love Him.

2. How's your campfire? Are you satisfied with its size? Why or why not?

3. John Stott once said, "Apathy is the acceptance of the unacceptable."[8] Have you ever been apathetic towards growing in your relationship with God?

4. Are you ready to start your half marathon? Are you ready to consider everything a loss compared with the surpassing greatness of knowing Jesus Christ? Take some time to evaluate your own desire for God before you answer.

5. What do you personally need to do to put another log on the fire and begin to fall more in love with God?

12 Texting God

In Matthew 5:6, Jesus makes this promise:

> "Blessed are those that hunger and thirst after righteousness, for they will be filled."

Because God's promises are always true, if you desire to build a bonfire and to fall more and more in love with God, He will help you do exactly that. But He won't just blast you with a lightning bolt that will make you know and love Him more. Desire has to be followed by action. I could sit on my couch all day desiring to eat some chocolate chip cookie dough ice cream. However, if I don't get up and go to the freezer, I won't ever eat any of that yummy treat. In the same way, your desire to love God more has to be followed by the willingness to do whatever it takes to actually experience that love.

But what does it take to fall more in love with God? Maybe you do want to love Him more, but you are a little hazy on where to start. Though it sounds somewhat complicated, it's really not. To grow in your love for someone, you have to get to know him or her better. So to learn to love God more, you hang out more with Him. Now, granted, this looks a little different from getting to know the girl sitting beside you in Chemistry. You can't literally hang out with God at a café and talk over a cappuccino. You can't text God or leave comments on His facebook. So how do you actually hang out with God and get to know Him more?

As a little girl, I remember playing with my Barbie dolls. I had the whole Barbie city—the McDonald's, the swimming pool, the department store, the apartment, and the beauty salon. I also had the incredibly cool Barbie corvette and van (which somewhat resembled the Mystery Machine in Scooby Doo), so I could take my Barbies wherever they wanted to go. I spent hundreds of hours with those dolls. I took them for baths in the bathroom sink, gave them real haircuts (which I later regretted), and even gave them first and last names. I still remember that my two favorite girl names were Summer and Autumn, and I dreamed of giving one of those names to my daughter. I guess I really liked seasonal names!

Anyway, I hung out a lot with those Barbies, but did I ever really get the chance to know them? Of course not! No matter how many times I held Barbie and Ken by the legs and made them confess their love for each other, they still couldn't actually talk. I could talk to them, and tell them all about myself, but they could never tell me anything about themselves. They weren't able to do that because they were pieces of plastic. They weren't alive. Despite the number of hours I spent with them, I would never get to know them. Thankfully, spending time with God is not like spending time with Barbie dolls. He is very much alive, and He can communicate with you in a variety of different ways. Because He wants you to know Him more, hanging out with Him can change your life.

Let's start with the obvious. One way to get to know Him better is by reading more of His Word, the Bible. I realize that some of you who have been raised in church are now beginning to tune out. Although you may have heard it all before, hearing it and doing it are two different things, so please stay tuned in! The first four books of the New Testament (commonly called the Gospels) tell the story of Jesus' life while He was here on earth. Now if we Christians are to imitate Christ, wouldn't it be a good idea to find out how he lived? That just makes sense, doesn't it? The entire Bible reveals who God is—His character, His heart, His power, His faithfulness, His passion, His compassion. Inside my Bible, on the first page, I have written these words: "To: Lacei, From: God." The Bible was written for you as a means to help you discover who God is and to get to know Him better.

So, if you claim to be a Christian who wants to learn to love God with all her heart, reading it is not an option. It's not just a nice thing to do if you have time and it fits into your schedule. It's not something you do only when you feel like doing it. Reading God's word, when done with the right motives and desire, will give you life. It will give you guidance, comfort, direction, peace, whatever God knows that you need. As I mentioned before, Hebrews 4:12 says,

> "FOR THE WORD OF GOD IS ALIVE AND POWERFUL. IT IS SHARPER THAN THE SHARPEST TWO-EDGED SWORD, CUTTING BETWEEN SOUL AND SPIRIT, BETWEEN JOINT AND MARROW. IT EXPOSES OUR INNERMOST THOUGHTS AND DESIRES." (NLT)

The Bible is alive, and He uses it to both speak to us and to reveal Himself to us. It's not rocket science, girls. If you want to know God better, read His Word.

Now, some people seem to have the idea that the more they read, the better. So, they will zoom through ten chapters a day and feel really good about their time with God. But, if you ask them what they learned from those ten chapters, they don't have a clue. You shouldn't read the Bible just so that you can get through it; you should read it in order to learn or gain something from it. What do you expect when you read God's word? **EXPECT GOD TO SHOW YOU SOMETHING FROM HIS WORD, AND YOU WILL RECEIVE MUCH. DON'T EXPECT ANYTHING, AND YOU WON'T RECEIVE MUCH OF ANYTHING.**

So how do you read the Bible with right expectations? There are many different methods that people use for studying the Bible. Some like to read using the SOAP method.[9] You pick a SCRIPTURE that stood out to you during your reading. Then you OBSERVE it for what you believe it means in the context. Next, you APPLY it to your life. Last, you PRAY about it. Other people simply read until something makes them stop. Maybe it's a verse that stood out that applies to their current situation. Maybe it's just something they've never noticed before. Maybe it's a story they read that intrigued them or challenged them to make a change. Other people like to use devotional books to help with their

Bible reading. The idea is that you just take the time to stop and study God's word. You have to allow Him time to speak through it. You have to expect that He will show you something.

I would strongly advise you to journal what God has been showing you on a consistent basis. I realize that this is somewhat difficult for some, but I feel the benefits outweigh the inconvenience. For myself, I don't always remember what happened yesterday, much less what God showed me a week ago! Journaling forces me to make the effort to actually put into words what God's been up to in my life. If I had decided not to take notes in one of my college classes because it wasn't really necessary, I would have done poorly in the class. I wouldn't have been able to remember much of what the professor was trying to teach me. It is true that I possibly could have squeaked by and passed the class, but I wouldn't have got as much out of it, and I couldn't have gone back later and reviewed what I'd been taught. By journaling what God shows me on a consistent basis, I know exactly what He's been teaching me yesterday, today, and two years ago. I can look back over

Scripture
Pick out a verse or two that stood out to you.

Observation
What's going on here? What is being said in your own words?

Application
What should I do with this? How do I live this out?

Prayer
Write a prayer asking God to help you apply what you've learned. Say thanks for His word.

the past year and be amazed at how much more I've learned about Him—at how far He's taken me.

Let me just make a little interjection here because sometimes students get discouraged when I mention journaling. They feel that since they didn't have any huge revelation from their Bible reading, they don't have anything to write about in their journal. Let me be extremely honest and encourage you a little. There are times when you will have those lightning bolt experiences with God's Word—when the words on the page seem to glow and you are hit with an amazing revelation. There are also times when what you read seems to directly speak to you personally.

But there are other times when it's not so much of a revelation as it is a confirmation. It's simply a reminder of how cool God is. Just today, during my time with Him, I read the story of Jesus walking on the water in John Chapter 6. I noticed that verse 31 says that when He got into the boat with the disciples, "immediately the boat reached the shore where they were heading."

My journal entry was simply an exclamation of how cool Jesus is: I wrote, "You calmed the storm and saved some travel time, just because you can!" It wasn't some big, deep theological revelation, but it did help remind me of who Jesus is—the incredibly amazing, all-powerful God of the universe. **THOUGH NOT EVERY DAY YOU SPEND TIME WITH HIM IS A LIGHTNING BOLT EXPERIENCE, EACH DAY BUILDS ON THE LAST, AND EVERY DAY IS IMPORTANT TO FALLING MORE IN LOVE WITH HIM.**

As far as where to read, some like to read in several places at once while others like to stick to one book at a time. If you do read in several places as once, I would suggest putting bookmarks in each of those sections—maybe one in the Old Testament, one around Psalms or Proverbs, one in the gospels, and one somewhere else in the New Testament. It's good to have continuity in where you are reading so that you understand the context of the writing—who the writer is, who he is writing to, the historical background. Knowing that kind of information before reading a book of the Bible can shed a whole lot of light on some Scripture and cut down on those "Huh?" moments. Many study Bibles include that kind of background information which is far easier than trying to figure it all out yourself. If you consistently open your Bible and read wherever it lands, you will miss out on some of that context. So wherever you read, be an educated reader.

Obviously, you can get to know God through reading His Word, but that's not the only way you get to know Him. You can also learn who He is by simply experiencing Him, by making yourself available to Him. One way to do this is to make time for you two to simply be together. You have a hang-out time with God. You spend time talking with Him, telling Him how you feel, how your day was, thanking Him for His blessings. You spend time worshiping Him (with or without music), praising Him for who He is. You spend time asking Him for direction and help with your needs and the needs of others.

Then you take time to listen. If you talk to Him, He will talk back. But He doesn't always talk in quite the same way we do. He's not limited to the confines of human communication. Sometimes He doesn't even use words. He might just decide to respond by giving you that feeling of peace, joy, or courage that only He knows you need. He might respond by just wrapping His arms around you and holding you in

His lap for awhile, reassuring you that you will make it. But other times, He will talk back with words, spoken through the Holy Spirit who lives inside of you.

As you make conversations with God a part of your life and walk beside Him on this journey, you will never cease to be amazed at how incredible He is—at how overwhelmingly in love He is with you, at how awesomely powerful He is, at how totally faithful He is, at how indescribably peaceful your life can be. As you spend time talking with Him, you experience Him answering your prayers and talking back to you in a way that's hard to put into words. But you won't be able to hear His voice if you won't take the time to chat with Him. So make the time. He's worth listening to, and you will grow to love Him even more because of it.

Another way you make yourself available to Him is to make the most of every opportunity that you're given. For instance, if you have the opportunity to be in a small group of girls your age who can voice their questions and who can be encouraged, prayed for, and challenged by a godly leader, you do it. If you have the chance to spend more time in prayer around the altars after a service, you take it. If you have the opportunity to listen to God's Word spoken through His messenger (like your youth pastor or leader), you pay attention and remain sensitive to what God wants to say to you. If you are blessed to have people in your life who could be godly mentors for you, you spend time with them. Ask them to go out for ice cream (my personal favorite), ask them questions, and learn from their wisdom. If you have the opportunity to go to a place where you can worship with others, you don't take that for granted. You put the distractions aside, get past the way you might feel, and you worship God because He simply deserves it. If you have the chance to serve others—whether on a trip overseas, in a soup kitchen, at your school, or in your own home, you take it. By making the most of every opportunity you're given, you make yourself available for Him to move in your life. By experiencing Him moving in your life, you will get to know Him and love Him more.

As you fall more and more in love with Him, something very interesting happens. You will want to follow His guidelines for how to live your life. Jesus says in John 14:15,

"If you love me, you will obey my commands."

I realize that even as I mention this, there might be a few of you that may think, "Okay, here comes all the rules." But that's not the case whatsoever. As I mentioned before, following rules does not make you a Christian. As you fall more in love with Him, you realize that the guidelines He set for you in Scripture are for your own good. They are written not out of anger or punishment but out of love. Just as a parent gives a child rules to protect her from oncoming traffic or an unguarded swimming pool, our heavenly Dad tells us ways we can also protect ourselves from hurt and prevent hardship throughout our lives. Because I know that He knows a whole lot more about life than I do, I choose to listen to Him. Because I know He loves me and has my best interests in mind, I choose to trust Him for guidance. Because I simply love Him, I choose to obey His commands.

The more you take the time to hang out with God, the more you'll realize who He is, the better you'll know Him, and the more in love you'll fall with Him. But just as I didn't reach the level of love I have right now for my husband overnight, your love for God should also change over time—if you take the time to get to know Him. Just as my husband and I had to choose to make time for each other so that our love would grow stronger, you must also choose to make time for Him. As you spend time getting to know Him and experiencing how good He truly is, you can't help but love Him more. So, put that other log on your fire, and get ready to build a bonfire. It's a decision you will never regret, and the results are indescribable.

Hebrews 4:12

"For the word of God is alive and powerful. It is sharper than the sharpest two-edged sword, cutting between soul and spirit, between joint and marrow. It exposes our innermost thoughts and desires." (NLT)

Reflection Questions

1. How well do you feel you know God? Do you feel close to Him?

2. Why do you sometimes feel closer to God? Why is that important? Is God there when you don't feel Him?

3. How can you get to know Him better?

4. Do you have trouble wanting to read your Bible? If so, why do you think that is?

5. How do you read the Bible? What are your expectations?

6. How do you have a conversation with God? How does that actually work in your life?

7. How do you make yourself available to God?

8. Why does God give us commands to follow?

13 Picking up Grapes

Jesus teaches us that being a Christian is all about loving God and loving people. But in my own life, I've found it far easier to love an amazingly perfect God than it is to love His creation who are far less than perfect. How easy is it for you to love people? For most of us, that depends on who the person is. It's probably fairly easy to love your best friends, maybe your mom or your dad. But how easy is it for you to love that guy in Algebra that calls you names that you don't even want to repeat? How easy is it to love that girl in your neighborhood who spread that nasty rumor about you? What about that ex-boyfriend who acted like a jerk? Why in the world would you want to love them? It doesn't make much sense, does it? It makes a lot more sense simply to love those who love us and treat badly those who treat us badly.

Interestingly enough, God speaks to this kind of logic quite a few times in His Word. In Matthew 5:44, Jesus instructs,

> "Love your enemies and pray for those who persecute you."

Then Paul writes this in Ephesians 4:32:

> "Be kind and compassionate to one another, forgiving each other, just as in Christ God forgave you."

John also discusses the same topic:

> "Anyone who claims to be in the light but hates his brother is still in the darkness. Whoever loves his brother lives in the light, and there is nothing in him to make him stumble. But whoever hates his brother is in the darkness and walks around in the darkness; he does not know where he is going, because the darkness has blinded him." (I John 2:9-11)

This is not easy stuff. Honestly, by ourselves, it is impossible stuff. **It's only with God's help that we can truly love those that aren't lovable and forgive those who seemingly don't deserve it.** It's only with God's help that we can actually see those around us through His eyes. Most of us have two obstacles we have to get over before we can learn how to fall in love with people—our past and ourselves.

Everyone has been hurt at some time in his or her life, usually multiple times. When I was in late elementary school, I went through a stage when I had a few more pounds than most of the other girls in my class. I remember the horror of fourth grade swimming lessons. We were herded into the locker room like cattle and given a colored swimsuit to match our sizes. I still remember that the skinny girls got blue, the medium-sized ones got yellow, and the bigger ones got red or green. I had to wear the red one, along with two or three other girls in my class, which made me feel like I was somehow inferior. I'm still not sure why in the world someone thought that giving sensitive fourth grade girls colored swimsuits by size was a good idea! Anyway, as you know, people can be cruel, and I still remember numerous times that comments were made about my weight. Even now, as I think about one particular adult that made fun of me and should have known better, I could let myself get mad at him all over again. But what good does that do me? It does me no good whatsoever.

In fact, it actually does me harm. Jesus tells us this in Matthew 6:14-15:

> "For if you forgive men when they sin against you, your heavenly Father will also forgive you. But if you do not forgive men their sins, your Father will not forgive your sins."

That means that if we don't forgive each other, He can't forgive us. You might say, "But what if that person that hurt me never asked for forgiveness? What if he or she doesn't deserve to be forgiven?" Let me ask you one question in response to the previous two: Does any of us deserve to be forgiven? I know I still mess up. I have at times made the same mistakes over and over again. I still have trouble consistently imitating Him. I don't deserve Him to forgive me either, but He does. According to C.S. Lewis, "To be a Christian means to forgive the inexcusable, because God has forgiven the inexcusable in you."[10]

I know that some of you may be thinking that getting made fun of is a walk in the park compared to what you've been through. Some of you have been hurt so badly that you can't even bring yourself to talk about it. Others of you have been so hurt that you've vowed to never again let yourself get too close to anyone. You have put up a wall around yourself to prevent you from further pain. You might even have a negative view of people in general, which makes it difficult to follow Jesus' command to love people.

If any of these describes you, I am truly sorry. Life here on this earth can be incredibly difficult sometimes. But no matter how big the wrong, you must let it go and learn to forgive. You've got to let go of the anger, the pain, and the grudge you hold against that person. That's not something that will happen overnight, but if you start the process of asking for God's help, it is possible. Ephesians 3:20 says,

> ". . . [He] is able to do immeasurably more than all we ask or imagine . . ."

It may be hard for you to imagine forgiving the person who hurt you. But if we allow Him to, God can do far more in us than what we think is possible.

One way to start the process of forgiving someone who has wronged you is to begin sincerely praying for him or her. I know it sounds insane, and it's probably the last thing you want to do for that person. But it's amazing how praying for someone can change your heart. Jesus modeled this as he hung on the cross. He looked down at those who had crucified him, who had tortured and mocked him and said,

> "Father, forgive them, for they do not know what they are doing." (Luke 23:34)

What an example of truly loving others, despite their actions! He knows how it feels to be betrayed, to be hurt, to be abandoned by those closest to you. He can help you get over your past. He can help you learn to forgive and love those who have hurt you.

The other huge obstacle to get over when it comes to loving people is the one and only you. We have to get over ourselves. From the time we are born, our natural desire is to be selfish. That's why I've had to teach my three wonderful children to share with others. What they already know how to do is to scream "mine," grab the toy, hit the other sibling who wants it, and run away. That's natural. Although as we get older, we are hopefully still not screaming "mine," we continue to fight our human nature and what our culture teaches us as well. We are taught to look out for #1 and to do what's best for us. I know I naturally want to do things that will help me succeed, that will help me be comfortable, that will make my life better. It's so easy to get wrapped up in my wants and my needs. It's so easy to lead a lifestyle of pleasing ourselves.

But Philippians 2:3-7 makes it clear that God teaches a far different lifestyle:

> "Do nothing out of selfish ambition or vain conceit, but in humility consider others better than yourselves. Each of you should look not only to your own interests, but also to the interests of others."

You see, many of us walk around with blinders on, and we don't even know it. I know I've been guilty of getting too caught up in my own problems, my own stress, my own busyness to see anyone's needs but my own. One day, I was at Wal-Mart with my three children. I normally try to go on a day when my two oldest are in school, but the fridge was empty, and so I had to go on one of their days off. I had already stopped my boys from playing football with various grocery items and my girl from throwing canned vegetables out of the cart. My four year-old had tried to climb the toilet paper shelf, and the boys had started annoying each other on purpose. On top of that, my eighteen-month-old daughter had decided that she preferred running around with her brothers instead of sitting in her seat, so she had tried to jump ship numerous times. Needless to say, I was ready to be done with my shopping.

I put myself in turbo drive and headed towards the produce. It was my final stop before the check-out line, so I was beginning to see the light at the end of the tunnel. Just as I was trying to decide if I wanted to pay $3 a pound for grapes, an elderly man not far from me mistakenly picked up a broken bag of grapes. Suddenly, there were grapes rolling everywhere. I tried not to step on them as I stopped my cart and glanced at the man. He had a strange expression of both surprise and frustration. In that moment, I had a decision to make. Was I going to stop and help this man, or was I going to make a beeline to the check-out and pretend like I didn't see what had happened? Honestly, everything in me wanted to turn my head and keep walking. After all, it wasn't really my problem. It was the problem of that elderly man and the Wal-Mart clean up crew. Besides, I deserved to head straight home and take a long break after that grocery shopping experience. But I knew that wasn't the right thing to do.

So, I quickly started to pick up the grapes that were around my feet. As I bent over to do so, I noticed that my older son had already knelt down to help. In that moment, he taught me a huge lesson about noticing people. I realized that my son wasn't wrapped up in his own agenda. In fact, he probably didn't even know what an agenda was. He simply saw someone who needed his help. But I was so busy worrying about my own needs that I was tempted to look past the needs of others. I was so wrapped up in my schedule, my issues, and my day that I almost chose to wear blinders. **In order to learn to love others, we have to get over ourselves and open our eyes to those around us.**

But how do you actually walk that out? How do you actually change your way of thinking and open your eyes to others? One way is to take the time to be a need finder and a need filler. Lately God's been teaching me this concept, and it's a pretty simple one. If we, as Christians, are to meet people's needs around us, we must first find out what those needs are. Pretty deep, huh? The point here is that you have to take the time out of your day to really see those around you. You have to take the time to create relationships with people.

Now, I'm not just talking about your best friends that you've known since first grade. In Matthew 5:46-47, Jesus asks,

> "If you love those who love you, what reward will you get? Are not even the tax collector's doing that? And if you greet only your brothers, what are you doing more than others? Do not even the pagans do that?"

It's easy to be a need finder and filler for those who love you, for those whom you're closest to. Even people who don't live for God do that. But it takes more effort to be a need finder and filler to people that you aren't as close to, to those that you might have never even noticed before. It takes looking beyond yourself—beyond your needs, your schedule, your life—and seeing how you can serve others. It takes learning that it's all about them—not you.

Let me give you a real life example of how this works. One of my neighbors, through talking with me, discovered that my husband was having knee surgery and would not be able to do much physical activity for a while. A couple of days after the surgery, our grass was getting tall, and I heard the sound of a lawn mower. My neighbor was mowing our yard. She found a need and filled it. Now if she would have been caught up in her own life and busyness, she would have never thought about the fact that Keith's surgery would prevent him from mowing. In fact, she might not have even known that he was having the surgery. But my neighbor isn't like that. She's all about finding and filling other people's needs. She's learned how to open her eyes to those around her.

Another way we can get over ourselves is to learn humility. Ephesians 4:2 says,

> "Be completely humble and gentle; be patient, bearing with one another in love."

But what is humility? What's it mean to be humble? Webster's defines it as "the absence of pride."[11] However, in many instances, pride is a good thing. We can be proud of a good grade on a paper, proud of winning a volleyball game, proud of getting a lead in the musical. These are all instances in which we can be proud in a positive way.

But there's also a negative side of pride that is defined as "an unduly high opinion of oneself; arrogance."[12] If a person has too much of this kind of pride, loving others will be next to impossible. People that struggle with this type of pride like to talk about themselves and their accomplishments. Though they may not say it, they feel like they are somewhat superior in some ways to those around them. Now granted, very few of us would like to admit that we struggle with this type of pride. No one wants to think of herself as being arrogant. But if I am entirely honest with myself, **I know there have been times when my own pride prevented me from loving others.**

I remember times when I've struggled with spiritual pride, times when I thought that I was somehow superior to others because of my spirituality. I looked down on others who didn't know God like I did and who didn't follow His commands. Luke 18:9-14 makes it quite clear what Jesus thinks about this:

> To some who were confident of their own righteousness and looked down on everybody else, Jesus told this parable: "Two men went up to the temple to pray, one a Pharisee and the other a tax collector. The Pharisee stood up and prayed about himself: 'God, I thank you that I am not like other men—robbers, evildoers, adulterers—or even like this tax collector. I fast twice a week and give a tenth of all I get.'
>
> "But the tax collector stood at a distance. He would not even look up to heaven, but beat his breast and said, 'God, have mercy on me, a sinner.'
>
> "I tell you that this man, rather than the other, went home justified before God. For everyone who exalts himself will be humbled, and he who humbles himself will be exalted."

Instead of comparing myself to Jesus and seeing myself as I really was (a woman who still struggles to imitate Him), I compared myself to those around me. I acted just like the Pharisee in the parable. I looked down my nose at others in spiritual arrogance. When you do this, it is next to impossible to actually follow Jesus' command to love people.

To get past yourself and love others, you have to guard yourself against pride. You have to learn to see yourself properly. We all have weaknesses, and we all have strengths. Some of us have been blessed with the opportunity to learn about Christ. Some of us have not. Some of us still struggle with wanting to completely give our lives to Him. Some of us have already realized that we are created to live for Him.

Some of us still struggle with following certain commands, while some of us struggle with other ones. The one thing that we all have in common is that we are all sinners who have made mistakes. But some of us sinners have now decided to admit our mess-ups and to be saved by His grace. By seeing ourselves as we really are, we will be better able to see those around us as they really are. We will begin to see them through His eyes instead of our own.

The lyrics to Brandon Heath's song "Give Me Your Eyes" is a great example of what we should be daily praying as we seek to love people:

Give me your eyes for just one second.
Give me your eyes so I can see
Everything that I keep missing.
Give me your love for humanity.
Give me your arms for the broken hearted,
Ones that are far beyond my reach.
Give me your heart for the ones forgotten.
Give me your eyes so I can see.[13]

All of us need His eyes when it comes to loving people. But this doesn't come easily for most of us. Even the disciples struggled with seeing people as their teacher saw them. In Luke 18:15, the disciples rebuked the people who were bringing children to Jesus. Maybe the disciples felt as if the children wasted Jesus' time. After all, in many cultures, even today, children are considered the lowest in terms of their importance to society. They can't do very much yet, and they can't give much back to society. But Jesus didn't see them in terms of what they could do or give back. He simply adored and enjoyed them. He saw them in terms of what He could give to them.

Too often, I know that I've been guilty of seeing people in terms of how they can affect me instead of how I can affect them. I've tried at times to steer clear of people who I thought were draining, who were "lost causes", who were (what I considered) lacking socially or spiritually. Since those types of people didn't give anything back to me, I tried to not spend much time around them. Instead, I needed to see those people through His eyes. I needed to ask myself what I could give to them, not what they could give to me.

The same night that Jesus washed the disciples' feet (including Judas'), He made this statement:

> "A new command I give you: Love one another. As I have loved you, so you must love one another. By this, all men will know that you are my disciples, if you love one another." (John 13:34)

Jesus modeled what it meant to love people, regardless of what they could give back or do for Him. He knew that very night Judas would betray Him, Peter would deny knowing Him, and the others would run away in fear. Yet He still saw them for what He could give them, and He humbly served them, realizing that He would get nothing in return. **Seeing people through His eyes is taking all eyes off of yourself.** It is seeing people in terms of how you can serve them.

Loving imperfect people is not an easy task, but it is not an impossible one. As you learn how to get over the obstacles of your past and yourself, you will begin to show love to those around you—not just because you should, but because you have truly fallen in love with people.

Philippians 2:3-4

"Do nothing out of selfish ambition or vain conceit, but in humility consider others better than yourselves. Each of you should look not only to your own interests, but also to the interests of others."

Reflection Questions

1. When it comes to loving people, which obstacle is harder for you to get over–your past or yourself? Why?

2. Who are the hardest people for you to love?

3. Think about a time when you had trouble loving someone who hurt you. Did you learn to forgive him or her? How?

4. Why is pride (arrogance) such an obstacle when it comes to loving others?

5. How do you guard against a prideful attitude?

6. How can we see people through His eyes?

7. What is one thing that you have done recently that put others needs before your own?

Part 4: Who Am I Created to be?

14 Playing Prisoner

It should all be coming into focus now. You've cleaned off the dirt from the lenses, you've had your frames adjusted, and you are beginning to see more clearly. Now you are ready for your new prescription. You are ready to take a glimpse at who you were created to be through a new set of glasses—His glasses.

I recently read a quote by Anne Lamott that caught my attention: "My deepest belief is that living as if you are dying sets us free."[14] How would you live your life differently if you knew that you only had one week left on this earth? If you're anything like me, I would guess that you wouldn't waste one minute of those 10,080 minutes that you had left. You would make that week count and make the most of your last moments on earth! No one wants to end her life filled with regret over all the things she didn't do, yet it happens to many people. As I mentioned in the introduction to this book, I think one of the saddest events in life is when dying people realize that they forgot to truly live. Imagine how difficult it would be to discover, at death's door, that you had been so busy doing life that you never really lived. How traumatic to realize that you led an unfulfilled and unproductive life! How horrifying to know that you actually died long before your heart stopped pumping and your lungs stopped taking in air!

I am passionate about living my life with no regrets. I don't want to find myself lying on my death bed, wishing that I would have done more or feeling guilty about how I used the time I was given. I want to make a difference in my world now. I want to leave a legacy because of how I've impacted those around me. I want my life to be what it could be and should be according to Him!! I am guessing that you feel the same way. So how could and should your life be? What did God create your life to be like? How were you intended to live?

Isaiah 40:31 promises,

> "But those who hope in the Lord will renew their strength. They will soar on wings like eagles; they will run and not grow weary, they will walk and not be faint."

We were meant to soar. Have you ever had the opportunity to watch an eagle fly? Eagles look so majestic, so graceful, so confident as they effortlessly glide over the tops of the highest trees and mountains. They seem so peaceful, so sure that they are doing exactly what they were created to do. When God created our inmost being, when He knit us together in our mother's womb, He created us with intention. He didn't just throw some body parts together and say, "Well, that should work okay." He knit us together. I don't know if you've had much experience with knitting, but my aunt once taught me how to crochet. Believe me, it's a long and tedious process that takes a lot of patience! God didn't take nine months in creating us so that we could just make it through life, so that we could crawl along and eventually arrive at the end. He took His time creating us because we are made to soar just like eagles. He intentionally created us for a life of freedom.

How many times have you heard that Jesus came to set you free? Likely, you've heard it too many times to count. In Luke 4:18-19, Jesus reveals His purpose in coming to earth:

> "The Spirit of the Lord is on me, because he has anointed me to preach the good news to the poor. He has sent me to proclaim freedom for the prisoners and recovery of sight for the blind, to release the oppressed, to proclaim the year of the Lord's favor."

Jesus came so that we would no longer have to be in bondage to whatever is holding us captive. Yet I know that at times I've lived in anything but freedom. I've also heard stories of other Christians who have tried to escape their captor but can't seem to get free. How do you explain that?
2 Corinthians 3:17 proclaims,

> ". . . where the Spirit of the Lord is, there is freedom."

So, why do so many followers of Christ seem to be unable to truly walk in complete and total freedom?

I believe that one of the reasons for our lack of freedom is that it is simply easier to walk back into our prison cell. Even though it is cold, dark, and uncomfortable, we are familiar with it. We know exactly what will happen when we are there. For example, when I was held captive by fear, I knew exactly how to live in that bondage. I knew how to play the part of a prisoner. I had simply resigned to the fact that I was terrified to be alone and that I would be like that for the rest of my life. I reasoned that I had experienced a traumatic event as a middle schooler (having my house robbed), and so I would always struggle with feeling unsafe and vulnerable. I knew how to lie in bed with my heart racing, listening to each sound and trying to rationalize what it was. I knew how to make myself feel somewhat more at ease by searching every room and then trying to read or watch TV until I was tired enough to fall asleep quickly. I knew how to be held captive.

It seems that there is no shortage of captors in the world today. I've heard stories of people who have been held captive by an addiction to what makes them feel good—drugs, sexual acts, lustful thoughts, alcohol, pornography, overeating. I've also heard stories of people, especially girls, who are held captive by a negative perception of themselves. **SOME OF THESE GIRLS WILL DO ANYTHING TO FEEL BETTER ABOUT WHO THEY ARE.** They may starve themselves or try to throw up, date anyone that shows them attention, and go along with whatever the crowd wants to do just to be well-liked. Girls who are prisoners to this captor always compare themselves to others (and always find themselves lacking) which often leads to depression. I also know people who are held captive by a fear of failure. I once struggled so much with this captor that I wouldn't try anything unless I knew I could succeed. Obviously, my obedience to the Holy Spirit's leading was affected. I certainly wasn't willing to step out in faith and trust Him to do something that I couldn't already do in my own power. Still other people are held captive by unforgiveness; they are unwilling to let go of the anger they have held for so long. Others can't escape the fear that something bad is going to happen to someone they love. But no matter the captor, I know that it is easy to become accepting of that prison cell. Sometimes even the thought of trying to escape seems too distant and futile. But the fact remains that God created you for a life of freedom. A life in captivity is not how your life could and should be.

So how do you walk through that prison door? How do you get free? First of all you have to understand that freedom is never won without a fight. Our nation won its freedom in a rather large fight called the American Revolution. Later, slavery in our country was ended in another big fight called the Civil War. We won our freedom from having to pay the price for our sins through Jesus' fight and triumph over death. Freedom follows a fight. The word "freedom" actually means that you are "liberated from the control of some other person or some arbitrary power."[14] So, you can rest assured that the other power that is holding you captive is not going to just let you go easily. You have to be willing to put up a fight. Remember that anything worth having is worth fighting for.

"But," you may thinking, "I have no idea how to fight!" Maybe you don't even know how to throw a punch. My husband once tried to teach me how to punch, and he gave up; he said I hit like a girl. Go figure! Anyway, even if you are like me and don't have much experience in physical combat, you have to believe that you have the power within you to fight a spiritual battle. It's not about what you can or can't do in the fight. **It's about what He can do through you, and He always wins His fights.** Some people can't believe that they actually have that power. They have been telling themselves for so long that they are addicted to this, fearful of that, and struggle with everything in between that they have come to accept slavery as their identity. They accept those areas of bondage as part of themselves, as part of who they were meant to be. Simply put, that is a horrendous lie of the enemy.

> "Christ has set us free to live a free life. So take your stand! Never again let anyone put a harness of slavery on you." (Galations 5:1, MSG)

God created you to be powerful. He didn't create you to be satisfied with life as a prisoner. Look at 2 Timothy 1:7:

> "For God has not given us a spirit of fear and timidity, but of power, love, and self-discipline." (NLT)

You have the power within you to win the fight, but if you don't believe it, you will never experience that power, His power. But let's say you do believe it. You know that you are being held captive by something, and you believe that you have the power to fight this battle. What then?

You take action. You actually prepare yourself for battle. You recognize who you are fighting, and you start putting on your battle gear. You use Ephesians 6:10-18 as your battle plan.

> "A final word: Be strong in the Lord and in his mighty power. Put on all of God's armor so that you will be able to stand firm against all strategies of the devil. For we are not fighting against flesh-and-blood enemies, but against evil rulers and authorities of the unseen world, against mighty powers in this dark world, and against evil spirits in the heavenly places. Therefore, put on every piece of God's armor so you will be able to resist the enemy in the time of evil. Then after the battle you will still be standing firm. Stand your ground, putting on the belt of truth and the body armor of God's righteousness. For shoes, put on the peace that comes from the Good News so that you will be fully prepared. In addition to all of these, hold up the shield of faith to stop the fiery arrows of the devil. Put on salvation as your helmet, and take the sword of the Spirit, which is the word of God. Pray in the Spirit at all times and on every occasion. Stay alert and be persistent in your prayers for all believers everywhere." (MSG)

Some of you have been ineffective in battle for too long. You are wearing the helmet of salvation and the body armor of righteousness which have kept you alive through some of the attacks. But you can do so much more. You can actually move! You can move your shield to block Satan's shots. You can even go on the offensive and throw some punches by using the sword of the spirit—God's word. I remember pacing the hall of my house, praying for peace over my mind and my home, quoting and reading scripture after scripture as I continued to fight my battle against fear. I don't know how many times I quoted Psalms 4:8:

> "I will lie down and sleep in peace for you alone, Oh Lord, make me dwell in safety."

You see, even though I had already recognized my captor and asked Christ to give me freedom from it, I still had to walk in that freedom. I still had to take action and believe that I could continue to stay away from that prison cell. I told myself—out loud—that I was powerful, that I could do all things through Him who strengthens me, that when I am weak He is strong, that Satan has no power over me, that the demons tremble at the sound of the name of the Lord. I made an even greater effort to stay completely connected to the One who gave me the power I needed to do battle. I chose to fight for my freedom, and I won. Rather, He won. You see, God is not only waiting for us to fight, but also to learn that only He can actually win the fight. I John 4:4 reassures us that we have power to win the battle against the enemy:

> "You, dear children, are from God and have overcome them, because the One who is in you is greater than the one who is in the world."

God always trumps Satan.

It's so much easier to just run back to that prison cell, shut the door, and convince yourself that this is the way your life will be. **But God did not create you to live your life in captivity.** You must open that prison cell door and step out into the unfamiliar, but incredible world of freedom. It's only then that you will experience all that your life could and should be.

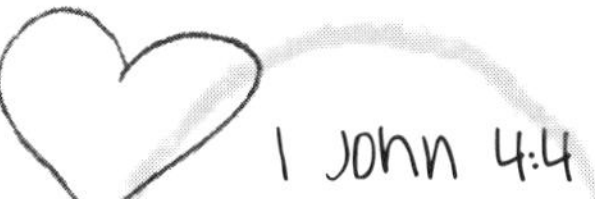

1 John 4:4

"You, dear children, are from God and have overcome them, because the one who is in you is greater than the one who is in the world."

Reflection Questions

1. If you really did know that you only had one week left on this earth, what would you do? How would you live differently?

2. Is there something in your life that you are being (or have been) held captive to? What is your captor?

3. Do you want to be free? If so, how do you stay out of the prison?

4. Why is it sometimes tempting to just accept your prison and learn to live with your captor instead of fighting?

5. Do you think you are powerful in spiritual battle? Does the enemy see you as a warrior or as a weakling? Why?

15 Making Lemonade

Not only are eagles free, but they also smile all the time. What? You don't believe me? Okay, so I don't know that to be a fact, but why wouldn't they smile? Eagles can effortlessly glide above mountains and waterfalls, and they have to be one of the most regal looking birds that God created. To top that off, they are the mascot of an entire country! Yeah, I'm sure that eagles must be joyful. And God created us to soar just like them.

In I Thessalonians 5:16, Paul instructs us to "be joyful always." This scripture used to make me kind of laugh and think, "Yeah, right." It conjured up images of the seven dwarfs whistling, "Heigh ho, heigh ho, it's off to work we go." I thought that Paul must have gotten confused and thought he was writing solely to fairy tale characters. After all, who could actually be joyful all the time? Let's say you just had a really bad morning. You woke up with a huge zit on your forehead, had an argument with your mom, flunked your Chemistry final, and dropped a ten-pounder on your thumb in weight training. **So, you are now supposed to skip to your locker with a big cheesy smile and proclaim the wonderful day you are having?** It seems a little strange, doesn't it? Anyone who acted like that would quickly be labeled a "weirdo." So what does Paul mean by "be joyful always?"

First we need to define what is meant by the word "joy." In this context, I don't believe that it is just a feeling. It is not a fleeting emotion that comes or goes depending on life's circumstances. Just recently, my two-year old daughter did this really cute little dance. She put her pointer fingers up beside her head and did a little disco move while she sang, "Me happy, me happy, me happy!" As a mother, I felt somewhat proud of helping her have such a positive outlook on her life. Yet, just as I began to feel really good about my accomplishment, within a couple minutes, the song stopped and she was throwing a fit about something one of her brothers had done. Emotions come and go, but true joy should remain (even when your siblings annoy you on purpose). **Joy is being content despite what is going on around you. It is choosing to maintain a right attitude, a right perspective about life regardless of how it's going.** It is an extremely difficult choice, and when life is going badly, it is a choice that is possible only with God's help.

I've heard it said that attitude is 5% what happens to you and 95% how you react to it. That means that your attitude about your life is determined by you. Check out Habakkuk 3:17-18:

> "EVEN THOUGH THE FIG TREES HAVE NO BLOSSOMS, AND THERE ARE NO GRAPES ON THE VINES; EVEN THOUGH THE OLIVE CROP FAILS, AND THE FIELDS LIE EMPTY AND BARREN; EVEN THOUGH THE FLOCKS DIE IN THE FIELDS, AND THE CATTLE BARNS ARE EMPTY, YET I WILL REJOICE IN THE LORD! I WILL BE JOYFUL IN THE GOD OF MY SALVATION!"

Habakkuk chose to be joyful and to remain content in the midst of hardships.

What about you? When life gives you lemons, do you make lemonade? Do you more often count your blessings or your problems? Do you see the cup as half full or half empty? Have you learned how to choose to be joyful, or do you more often choose the opposite? In Philippians 4:12b Paul shares what he has learned:

> "I HAVE LEARNED SECRET OF BEING CONTENT IN ANY AND EVERY SITUATION, WHETHER WELL-FED OR HUNGRY, WHETHER LIVING IN PLENTY OR IN WANT."

Want to know his secret? In verse 13 he continues,

> "I CAN DO EVERYTHING THROUGH HIM WHO GIVES ME STRENGTH."

Paul learned that being content was a matter of choosing the right way to react to life's circumstances. Instead of throwing in the towel and giving up when life got difficult, he chose to rely on the One who could give him all the strength he needed to make it through each and every situation.

Choosing to be joyful doesn't mean that you put on a mask and hide how you really feel. You will have ups and downs. You will have hardships in your life. Some days, you may even wake up and not feel like facing yet another day. Being a Christian does not exempt you from that. But, you choose the way you will deal with those feelings. My husband recently read *The Hiding Place* with our son, and as I listened to the story, I was amazed at the existence of joy in Corrie Ten Boom and her sister Betsie while they were in the worst place on earth, the concentration camps. Although they were freezing, starving, and looking daily at cruelty and death, Betsie found reason to celebrate. The room where she stayed at the camp had such enormous amounts of fleas and lice that even the guard wouldn't set foot in it. Because of the lack of guards, she had much more freedom to share Christ and read her Bible aloud in that room. So, Betsie actually rejoiced in the fact that where she was living was crawling with bugs. She made the choice to find a reason to be joyful.[16]

As a Christian you are not guaranteed that you will never have tough times, but you are guaranteed that you will never walk through those times alone.

> "Never will I leave you; never will I forsake you." (Hebrews 13:5)

Even through our ups and downs, we have One who is always consistent. Count on Him, not on the ease of your life. Then, choose to eliminate the negative thoughts. Choose to think on the things mentioned in Philippians 4:8:

"SUMMING IT ALL UP, FRIENDS, I'D SAY YOU'LL DO BEST BY FILLING YOUR MINDS AND MEDITATING ON THINGS TRUE, NOBLE, REPUTABLE, AUTHENTIC, COMPELLING, GRACIOUS—THE BEST, NOT THE WORST; THE BEAUTIFUL, NOT THE UGLY; THINGS TO PRAISE, NOT THINGS TO CURSE. PUT INTO PRACTICE WHAT YOU LEARNED FROM ME, WHAT YOU HEARD AND SAW AND REALIZED. DO THAT, AND GOD, WHO MAKES EVERYTHING WORK TOGETHER, WILL WORK YOU INTO HIS MOST EXCELLENT HARMONIES." (MSG)

A number of years ago, I went through a season in my life when life was very difficult. **I DIDN'T EVEN LOOK FORWARD TO GETTING UP IN THE MORNING.** Actually, I looked forward to the end of the day because I could mark off another day on my calendar. Because of my health problems, I had actually convinced myself that I was probably going to die. I even went so far as to tell my husband that after I died he needed to make sure to find a new wife who would be a good mother to our son. Though my situation was difficult, I know now that I could have chosen to have a different perspective about life during that time. I felt sorry for myself, and I was blinded to all the blessings that God had given me. I could see only all the hardships, all the times that God didn't show up, all the hurt that I felt inside. I had lost all hope, and I could see the cup as only half empty.

Looking back on that time in my life, I now realize that God taught me more about joy during those six months than in the five years before that. I now somewhat understand what James was saying in 1:2-4:

> "Consider it pure joy, my brothers, whenever you face trials of many kinds, because you know that the testing of your faith develops perseverance. Perseverance must finish its work so that you may be mature and complete, not lacking anything."

Even though those times when God stretches you are not extremely fun, they are necessary and essential to form you into the woman that you are meant to be. Even though my life circumstances were tough, it could have hurt a whole lot less if I simply had changed my perspective and actually chose to live a life of joy, a life of contentment. That's the way your life could and should be. So don't be discouraged when life hands you lemons. Just learn God's recipe for making lemonade!

James 1:2-4

"Consider it pure joy, my brothers, whenever you face trials of many kinds, because you know that the testing of your faith develops perseverance. Perseverance must finish its work so that you may be mature and complete, not lacking anything."

Reflection Questions

1. What is joy?

2. Do you think that you are a joyful person? Would others say that you are joyful?

3. When you are having a bad day, how do you normally react? How easy is it to think about good things in the midst of hardship?

4. How do you choose to be joyful? How does that actually happen?

5. Why should we "consider it pure joy" when we are faced with hard times?

16 Growing Feathers

I have a newsflash for you: You are not created to live a boring life. Just as your life was not meant to lack freedom or joy, your life is also not meant to lack adventure. Aren't you glad about that? In fact, following the leading of the Holy Spirit is the ultimate adventure! It is better than climbing Mount Everest, repelling, sky diving, or riding a roller coaster. You never know what He will lead you to do, and you most definitely don't know where you are going to end up. By choosing to serve Christ, you sign up for life to the extreme. So why do there seem to be bored Christians out there?

It's because of the risks involved. In order to live this awesome life of adventure, you have to be willing to live dangerously. You must be willing to do whatever God tells you to do, whenever He tells you to do it. You have to be willing to walk by faith. What's that mean? It means that you obey

His voice and walk forward when there doesn't seem to be anything to walk on. It means you trust Him at His promises when all human logic says that those promises can't ever be fulfilled. In one of Mark Batterson's books *Wild Goose Chase*, he says, "Faith is not logical. But it isn't illogical either. Faith is theological. . . Logic questions God. Faith questions assumptions. And at the end of the day, faith is trusting God more than you trust your own assumptions."[17] **FAITH IS NOT WALKING IN TOTAL BLINDNESS. IT IS SIMPLY CHOOSING TO SEE THROUGH HIS EYES INSTEAD OF YOURS. IT IS CHOOSING TO WEAR HIS GLASSES.**

Living a life of adventure means that you are willing to be a Noah and build an ark when there is no sign of rain. It means that you are willing to be an Abraham and believe that if God says it, you and your ninety-year-old wife could have a child. It means that you are willing to be a Peter and throw your net back into the water one more time. Look at Luke 5:5-7. Simon Peter had pulled an all-nighter. He had been out fishing all night and came back with nothing. Then, Jesus came on the scene and told him to do something entirely illogical. He told Peter to let down the nets and try again. Think about that. Peter was a fisherman. He knew that the fish were long gone. Yet he said,

> "Master, we've worked hard all night and haven't caught anything. But because You say so, I will let down the nets."

Though it made no sense, Peter trusted Jesus' ability to work outside of human logic. That's when the miracle happened. That's when God's power is revealed—when you step out in faith and say, **"NO MATTER HOW CRAZY THIS MAY**

seem, I will do whatever You ask, whenever You ask." That's when you as a Christian become dangerous and begin to live your life the way it could and should be.

Unfortunately, too many Christians get stuck simply going through the motions. They are doing just enough to get by in their walk with Christ. They aren't living in sin, but they aren't completely living for Him either. That's when life as a Christian gets boring. For whatever reason, they are not willing to abandon everything and follow the Holy Spirit's leading. Think about the story of the rich young man that is told in Matthew 19.

> Now a man came up to Jesus and asked, "Teacher, what good thing must I do to get eternal life?"
>
> "Why do you ask me about what is good?" Jesus replied. "There is only One who is good. If you want to enter life, obey the commandments."
>
> "Which ones?" the man inquired.
>
> Jesus replied, "'Do not murder, do not commit adultery, do not steal, do not give false testimony, honor your father and mother,' and 'love your neighbor as yourself.'"
>
> "All these I have kept," the young man said. "What do I still lack?"
>
> Jesus answered, "If you want to be perfect, go, sell your possessions and give to the poor, and you will have treasure in heaven. Then come, follow me."
>
> When the young man heard this, he went away sad, because he had great wealth.

He walked away sad because he knew that he was not willing to give it all up—his life of comfort, his life of predictability, his life of financial security. He wasn't ready to embrace the unknown and trust that Jesus could give Him a life that was better than what he could give to himself. Because of his unwillingness, he missed out on the greatest opportunity ever known to man. Think about it. Jesus told him to "follow me." There were only a select few that Jesus said that to, and the ones who took him up on the offer became His disciples. They became men who spent almost every waking moment with the Creator of the Universe. They became men who were radically changed themselves, and then they radically changed the world as we know it.

The rich young ruler missed out on his opportunity to jump out of "doing just enough to get by" and live a life of adventure, to live his life the way it could and should be. I would imagine that there were many times that he looked back on his decision with regret. But you don't have to make that same mistake. Figure out what is holding you back, what is keeping you from living dangerously for God. Realize that nothing is worth missing out on the adventure that God has created you to live. Say "yes" to Jesus' invitation to follow Him, wherever He might take you. Then take a deep breath and get ready for the ride of your life!

God created us to soar like eagles. But have you ever seen eagles in captivity? They look so out of place, so bored, so unfulfilled, so dissatisfied with life in a cage. It's almost as if they know that they were created for so much more than life in captivity. They are simply not living the life they were intended for. They were intended to soar. Yet did you know that eagles aren't born with the ability even to lift themselves off of the ground? They are born with a type of downy covering that doesn't allow them to fly. They have to wait until they are a little older to actually grow feathers that they can use for flight. I believe that sometimes we get stuck, covered in downy stuff. We become satisfied with the way our life is and we lose sight of how our life could and should be. We forget about living a life of no regrets and we settle for just living. But God intends your life to be so much more. So, grow some feathers, jump off a mountain, feel the rush of the wind on your face, and discover what it feels like to soar! That's the life you were created to live.

Isaiah 40:31

"Those who hope in the Lord will renew their strength. They will soar on wings like eagles."

Reflection Questions

1. Do you feel like you are living your life to its full potential? Why or why not?

2. Do you now or have you ever been stuck "just doing enough to get by" in your relationship with Christ? How do you think you got there? How do you get out?

3. Corrie Ten Boom said, "Faith sees the invisible, believes the unbelievable, and receives the impossible."[18] What do you think about that? Do you have this kind of faith?

4. Has God ever asked you to do something that seemed illogical by human reasoning? What happened?

5. Are you entirely willing to live dangerously for God (to do whatever He says whenever He says it)? If not, what is holding you back?

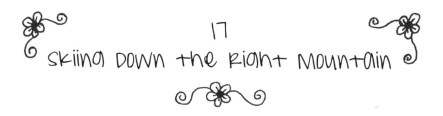

17
Skiing Down the Right Mountain

Have you ever met people who seem to be wandering aimlessly through life? They don't really have any idea about where they want to go, what they want to do with their life, or why they are even on the face of this planet. They are like a ball in a pinball machine. They just go wherever the flippers take them and bounce in whatever direction they are pushed towards. They are simply lost without a compass. Sadly, some of these people spend their entire life trying to discover what their purpose is, and they never live the life that they were created to live. Others begin believing that their life has no purpose, which leads them down a road of heartache and disappointment.

The truth is that you were created for a reason. God did not intend your days on Earth to be spent wandering around without direction. Remember Jeremiah 29:11?

> "'For I know the plans I have for you,' declares the Lord, 'plans to protect you and not to harm you, plans to give you hope and a future.'"

The God of the universe has plans for you! He has already drawn up a blueprint for your life, and He knows exactly how awesome your life could and should be. In Jeremiah 1:5, God says,

> "Before I formed you in the womb I knew you, before you were born I set you apart. . ."

That means that even before you were born, God had already determined His vision for your life, an amazing picture of freedom, joy, and adventure—a fabulous picture of what your life could and should be.

But how do you figure out what His vision is for your life? My senior year in high school, I agonized over this question. **I was so confused about what I should do with my life.** I really wanted to fulfill the plans that God had for me, but I had no idea where to start. When I was in middle school, I felt God tell me that I would someday be a foreign missionary. Then, for a while I wanted to be doctor (maybe medical missions), but my sophomore year I went on a rotation with some nurses in the emergency room. After turning green and nearly fainting while watching a little boy get stitches, I quickly concluded that was not God's vision for my life.

My junior year, I took psychology and decided that maybe counseling was the direction I should go. So I entered college as a psychology major. But, after working for a while as a youth leader at my church and loving it, I decided that

I would rather teach psychology to students than be a psychologist. So I switched to a social science education major. Then during my freshman year in college, my English professor approached me about changing my major to english education. I realized that my love for students and love for writing could actually both be fulfilled with that major, and so, after graduating, I became an English teacher.

Does that mean that I had fulfilled God's vision for my life? After landing that teaching job, could I have just sat back and said, "Okay, I'm done now. I have discovered Your vision, and now I can just sit back and relax"? Sometimes we think that God's vision for our life and our career choice are the same thing. As a high school student, I remember thinking that way. I couldn't wait to find out what job I was supposed to have so that I could quit agonizing over what God's plans were for my life. But God's plans—His vision for your life—is so much more than that. It doesn't all hinge on one decision of what your major should be (though you do need to seek Him earnestly for direction in making that choice). It doesn't all hinge on you hearing that one word about your future during altar time (though you should continually seek to hear His voice). **His vision is everything your life could and should be one day from now, three days from now, one year from now, ten years from now, and even twenty-five years from now.** His vision for your life is not something that is communicated with a few words. It's something that is said with an entire book.

I want you to pick up a fairly thick book and hold it in your lap. One of your textbooks would work fine, and I'm sure you have one of those lying around your room! Now, imagine that the book in your lap is God's vision for your life. It's everything that your life could and should be. On the front cover, God has written, "My plans for ______ (insert your name). In this book, there are pictures of you in your dorm room at college, your wedding day, your children, even pics of you at the age of 45! It tells you when you will meet Mr. Right, how he will propose, what career you will have, where you will live, who your close friends will be, what your children will grow up to be, whose lives you will impact, and everything in between. How badly do you want to open this book? How much would you pay for just one glimpse of its pages?

If you're anything like me, you would give nearly everything you have to open that book sitting on your lap. But let me let you in on a little secret. The book that symbolizes God's vision for your life is already open. You are now in the process of living it. When you gave your life to follow Him, you started chapter one. You started living out His vision—all that could be and should be true for your life. You see, God's vision is not just a destination, not just an occupation, not just something that you have to try to achieve. It's not something you figure out; it's something you live out. It's not that once you get to chapter 7, you are really in God's vision for your life, and there will be no more chapters. It's not that once you get to "it", you're done. As long as you are still breathing, you will still be writing chapters, and they will each be wonderfully different.

After I landed my dream job of teaching English in high school, I quickly discovered that I was pregnant with our son, and I decided to be a stay-at-home mom. (A new chapter began.) A year later, we felt as if we were supposed to go overseas as missionaries to youth in Benin, West Africa, so we resigned our youth pastorate in Missouri. (A new chapter began.) We traveled to different churches for a year, raised our support, and went to France to learn French (the national language of Benin). (A new chapter began.) A year later, we arrived in Benin. (A new chapter began.) Almost a year later, we came home on medical leave because of complications with my second pregnancy. (A new chapter began.) Six months later, God led us to begin a youth ministry in Indiana. (A new chapter began.) Five years later, we knew it was God's will to minister to youth in Michigan. (Yet another chapter began.)

If you let God write the chapters the way they are meant to be written, He will take you on an incredible journey. What you think God will have you do for the rest of your life may actually only be a chapter in the vision He has for you. The important thing is that you are walking with Him in each of these chapters. Sometimes He even gives you dreams and visions to help lead you to the "more" that He has already planned in the later chapters of your book. What an adventure we get to live as His daughters!

> "For we are God's masterpiece. He has created us anew in Christ Jesus, so we can do the good things He planned for us long ago." (Ephesians 2:10, NLT)

We are His masterpieces, His works of art, and He created us to walk with Him through each chapter of our life.

Just to let you know from experience, some chapters are a whole lot more fun than others! Some might even feel as if they are never going to end. But you will have to continue to faithfully walk with Him through each chapter of your life.

Though you may not be content with the chapter God has you in right now, and you may wish that this were a "Choose Your Own Adventure Book" (where you could decide to skip a couple chapters), each chapter of His vision is essential to the book as a whole. You can't skip ahead (though you may want to) because without just one of these chapters, the others wouldn't be possible. Each chapter builds on the next and prepares you for what's to come.

Think back to math in elementary school. Did you first learn how to divide before you learned how to add? Of course not! You had to learn to add before you could learn to multiply. Then you had to learn to multiply before you learned how to divide. So from kindergarten to second grade, you worked on your addition skills. Then in third grade, they threw in some multiplication and a little division. After that, you learned long division and how to do even more difficult problems. But in order to succeed in doing the skill that was necessary in the 3rd grade, you had to first succeed in doing your first grade work. In order to succeed in doing what God has for you to do in the future (in your chapter 10), you must first succeed in doing what he is asking you to do right now (in your chapter 3). **YOU MAY THINK THAT THE CHAPTER YOU'RE IN RIGHT NOW IS POINTLESS,** and you may be tempted to skim it and skip to the next chapter. But you can't do long division as a first grader. You have to realize that God's timing is always best, and he knows when your chapters should begin and end. He knows when you've mastered what He is teaching you now and when you are ready to move on to the next thing you need to learn.

God's vision for your life is not something that is hiding out there somewhere that you have to try to find. It's not a carrot dangling on the end of a stick that you have to figure out how to reach. You are not preparing for God's vision; if you are following Him, you are living it now. Isn't that awesome? Is that freeing for some of you? I know that it was for me. **Life is not a game of hide and seek, with God hiding this "thing" called His vision somewhere and then expecting you to continually look for it.** You don't have to search for it. You simply have to search for Him. Jeremiah 29:13 says,

> "You will seek me and find me when you seek me with all your heart."

If you are walking each day of your life striving to know, to love, and to serve Him, you won't wake up one day and discover that you are totally out of His plan for your life.

Think about it this way. Imagine you are skiing in the Swiss Alps (a nice thought!), and you are at the top of the mountain, trying to decide which slope to take. The one on your right is a double black diamond (for very experienced skiers), and the one on your left is a blue slope (for the average Joe). Being a little less than confident in your skiing ability, you decide to take the blue one. So which direction do you need to point your skis? If you point your skis left, will you go right instead? Of course not! Unless you fall off your skis and roll down the mountain, you will go only in the direction that your skis are pointed. So if your ski instructor is Jesus, you will not suddenly discover that you went down the entirely wrong mountain. As long as you are asking Him for direction, He will keep you on the right slope. He will help you live your life as it could and should be lived. He will guide you in how to fulfill His vision for your life today, tomorrow, and for the rest of your years.

Ephesians 2:10

"For we are God's masterpiece. He has created us anew in Christ Jesus, so we can do the good things He planned for us long ago." (NLT)

Reflection Questions

1. What do you think might be God's vision for your life (today, tomorrow, in the future)?

2. Have you ever (as I did) had a faulty understanding of His vision for your life? Have you seen it more as the light at the end of the tunnel, as what happens in the end of your book? Why did you see it that way?

3. Are you satisfied with the chapter you are in right now, or do you find yourself wishing to be in another chapter? What chapter are you most looking forward to?

4. What's the problem with skipping or skimming chapters in God's book for you?

5. How can you be assured that after making a decision, you won't end up skiing down the completely wrong mountain?

18 Protecting Your Book

Did you like borrowing His glasses for a while? Would you like to keep wearing them so that you can more clearly see yourself, your God, His followers, and His vision? Are you beginning to see a difference in the way you are viewing things now compared to how you saw things before? I sincerely pray that you are. You should now understand what the meaning of "God's vision" truly is. It's not a light at the end of the tunnel, or you achieving a certain "thing." It's you walking each day of your life as it could and should be. Yet how do you really live that way? How do you make sure that you are making the most of the life that you've been given? How do you know that you are living chapter four in such a way that you will make it to chapter fifteen? The answers to these questions are found in the following five principles. Live by them, and you will both protect your book and fulfill His vision for you.

1. Avoid spills. Unfortunately, God's plan for your life is not guaranteed to happen. You can't just assume that you will live out God's mental picture for your life. Just getting on the right mountain doesn't mean that you will live out God's vision for your life. Satan wants to do everything He can to make you take a wrong turn. First Peter 5:8 warns,

> "Be self-controlled and alert. Your enemy the devil prowls around like a roaring lion looking for someone to devour."

Satan would love to rip out chapter four of your life. He can't read it, but he knows that God's hand is on your life, and he knows that you are capable of doing great damage to his agenda. But, he can't take out any part of God's vision for your life. It's off limits to Him. What he can do is convince you to rip out the pages yourself.

You may be thinking, **"What? Why would I ever rip out any pages of God's plan for my life? I would never do that!"** If Satan directly asked you to take the beloved book that was on your lap and mess it all up, you would say "No way!" But Satan doesn't work like that. He doesn't ask you directly. He tries to trick you. 2 Corinthians 11:14-15 states,

> "Satan disguises himself as an angel of light... his servants also disguise themselves as servants of righteousness." (NLT)

He tries to convince you to make little choices that will begin to change the appearance of the writing on your pages. They seem insignificant, but they are actually affecting many of the chapters in your book—in God's vision of what your life could and should be. Satan's M.O. (his mode of operation) is to lie to you, to make you think that your bad choices are not a big deal, to reassure you that you can control the consequences and that everything will be all right.

Have you ever spilled your drink on a book that you were reading? Do you remember what happened to the pages of that book? Even after those pages dried, they were never exactly the same. They were somewhat warped and didn't lie as flat and smooth as they used to. If the drink was dark (like coffee), you may have noticed that the pages were somewhat stained. Some of the words may have been smudged and hard to read. Some of the pages may have even been torn while they were still wet. You see, spills distort not just one page in a book; they affect the following pages as well.

The same principle applies to day-to-day choices that you make. You can make choices today that will, in effect, spill things on God's vision for your life. You can smudge the plans of what God intended your life to be. And although you can clean up the spill and make things right with Him once again, your book will still be stained slightly. It will never be exactly the same. Even if you are several chapters past the spill, you will still be able to see the warped pages, and Satan will often try to remind you of exactly what you spilled. He enjoys throwing your past mistakes in your face, even if you have been forgiven of them. Like it or not, spills will affect your future.

So if you want to live out everything that God envisions for you, you will do all you can to avoid spills. But first you need to understand exactly what spills are. Spills are choices that will negatively affect your future. Sometimes, spills happen due to blatant sin. A dating couple allow themselves to be alone for far too long and can never again stand before their future spouses as virgins. A student decides to experiment with some illegal drugs and ends up spending the end of her senior year suspended instead of graduating with her friends. Another student cannot forgive the person who has hurt her and allows bitterness and anger to control her life. Yet another student is continually hateful and disrespectful towards her parents, ignoring their instruction and God's command to honor them. God's vision for all these lives—of everything good that might have been—is forever changed.

Other times, spills are not necessarily blatant sin, but they are choices that simply aren't the best. I've seen student after student think that he or she can handle dating someone who is not truly following Christ. Some think that they can missionary date and "win him to Jesus." Others think that the relationship is okay because he goes to church occasionally or "it's not like we are going to get married or anything." The process of dating itself is to find someone that you do want to marry, to discover if that guy is your Mr. Right. If you are serving God, let me assure you that your Mr. Right is also serving God. **So dating a guy who is not serving God is not only a waste of time, it's also a very dangerous road that can detour you from everything that your life could and should be.** God will not give you more than you can bear, but you can give yourself more than you can bear.

You don't want to rip pages out of this awesome book that God has written for you. You don't want to allow things to be spilled on the pages of all your life could and should be. So avoid spills at all costs. Don't even allow a drink to be in the same room as your book! It's not worth the price you will pay.

2. Stop making excuses. How many of you have ever thought or said this: "But, God, I'm just not old enough to do that yet"? It's not an uncommon thought. You are in good company. After God tells Jeremiah that he was chosen to be a prophet to the nations, Jeremiah exclaims,

> "Ah, Sovereign Lord, I do not know how to speak, I am only a child." (Jeremiah 1:6)

When Paul asks Timothy to stay and oversee the church in Ephesus, he must have known that Timothy might struggle with his inexperience. He says,

> "Don't let anyone look down on you because you are young, but set an example for the believers in speech, in life, in love, in faith, and in purity." (I Timothy 4:12)

When David volunteers to fight Goliath, King Saul replies,

> "You are not able to go out against this Philistine and fight him; you are only a boy, and he has been a fighting man from his youth." (1 Samuel 17:33)

All of these stories involve making people feeling insecure because of age, but let's take another look at the last one. David wasn't the one making excuses. David knew he was only a boy, but he also knew how big his God was. God doesn't look for people who are past a certain age. He looks for people who know that He can do anything, despite the circumstances.

What about this excuse? "God, I think you've made a mistake. She is way more talented than I am. Why don't you ask her to do it?" We all have insecurities. We all have things that we wish we were better at. But God doesn't only call us to do things that we are good at. **Actually, he often calls us to do things that we aren't so good at so that we will have to actually rely on Him.** It doesn't take much trust in Him to do something that we can do on our own. But, whenever He asks us to do something that we are not naturally capable of doing, we learn how to trust in Him completely. In the book of Judges, Gideon told God about one of his insecurities. God asked Him to lead an army, and he had never led anything in his life. He said he was even "the least in his family" (Judges 6:15). But Gideon still followed God's instructions, and he ended up defeating the whole Midianite army with a mere 300 men and no weapons. Sometimes God chooses you because you aren't good at what He's calling you to do. God doesn't call the equipped. He equips the called.

Here's another excuse that I know I've used: "God, I'm not sure if you noticed or not, but I'm really busy and stressed right now. I just don't have time to do that." Life will never come to a point when you feel like you aren't busy. You simply have to decide to make time for the things that are most important. If you don't make that decision, the things that are of less importance will take the pla those that are of most importance. Then, you will never live the life that God intended you to live. Instead of experiencing how it feels to soar above the highest mountains and view breathtaking waterfalls, you will be stuck in a zoo with your wings clipped, viewing the same sights day after day. Life does not just happen to you. Usually, you decide what happens. So decide to stop making excuses and live your life to its full potential. Get your priorities straight, and live life as it was meant to be lived.

3. Guard your circle of influence. Have you ever heard anyone say, "show me your friends, and I'll show you your future?" Basically, it means that your life will be either positively or negatively affected by the people you choose to be close to. At your age, I was a little skeptical of this statement. **I thought I was strong enough to stand for what I believed in, not to be swayed by the opinions and actions of my friends.** I found out that I was somewhat right and somewhat wrong. I was strong enough not to be swayed by friends whom I was close to, but not constantly around. I could have great relationships with these people, and I could even share my relationship in Christ with them. But those people whom I chose to be around a lot, those who were my closest friends (or boyfriends), greatly affected my decisions. Sometimes they helped me make wise choices, but other times they encouraged me to make bad choices. They had the power to influence me.

You must realize that if you are standing on a chair, and one of your friends is standing on the floor beside you, it is far easier for her to pull you down than for you to pull her up. Remember the story about Aaron? He was Moses' brother, his spokesperson. He saw Moses' staff turn into a snake. He saw the Red Sea part. He even ate the manna that God gave them from heaven. He had experienced God's power firsthand. Still, what did he do when he was surrounded by a bunch of his friends who were unhappy with God? He helped them make an idol, a fake god, to worship in place of the Lord. Talk about being swayed by the crowd!

But what would have happened if Moses had been there when the people asked Aaron to make the idol? Would he have still done it? I think not. He would have had someone there to help him make the wise decision, to encourage him to do what was right in God's eyes. We all need to have a Moses (or two or three) in our lives. You need to have someone who's got your back—someone who can encourage you when you are weak and give you a loving push in the right direction. You need godly friends. You are not meant to try to serve God on your own. Proverbs 27:17 makes that point:

> "As iron sharpens iron, so one man sharpens another."

You also need to have people you can look up to as role models, as examples of what living for God is all about. If you don't have a Moses in your sphere of influence, find one. The pages of your book will have far fewer stains because of it.

4. Expect hardship. Living God's vision for your life will not be easy. Thomas Aquinas once said, "To one who has faith, no explanation is necessary. To one without faith, no explanation is possible."[19] You will be misunderstood. You will most likely be laughed at and ridiculed. In certain countries, you could even be thrown into prison. Jesus guaranteed that you would be persecuted:

> ". . . If they persecuted me, they will persecute you also . . ." (John 15:20)

Sounds like fun, huh? No one enjoys hardship. No one likes going through difficult times, but by being prepared for them, you can better endure.

After God called Jeremiah to be a prophet and declare His word to the nations, He said,

> "Get yourself ready! Stand up and say to them whatever I command you. Do not be terrified by them, or I will terrify you before them. Today I have made you a fortified city, an iron pillar and a bronze wall to stand against the whole land—against the kings of Judah, its officials, its priests and the people of the land. They will fight against you but will not overcome you, for I am with you and will rescue you." (Jeremiah 1:17-19)

God gave Jeremiah a heads-up: "They will fight against you." As you read through Jeremiah's life, you see that his own family betrayed him and cried out against him. He was beaten and put in stocks. He was even thrown into a well and left for dead. But Jeremiah continued to do what God called Him to do. He continued to live God's vision for His life. He not only had the heads-up, but he also knew that God keeps His promises. He knew that if God said He would rescue him, He would rescue him!

Although you can expect hardship, God promises to give you all you need to make it through those difficult times.

> "His divine power has given us everything we need for life and godliness through our knowledge of Him who called us by His own glory and goodness." (2 Peter 1:3)

He also can use those hard times to mold you into the woman you need to be.

> "Though now for a little while you may have had to suffer grief in all kinds of trials. These have come so that your faith . . . may be proved genuine." (1 Peter 1:6-7)

So expect to go through hard times, but also allow God to make the most of them. We are often most moldable when we are broken. Although it's more comfortable when life is easy, keep in mind this anonymous proverb: **"Smooth seas do not make skillful sailors."**

5. Seek to Hear from Him. If you are going to live out God's vision, you have to stay in contact with the author of your book. You have to listen to what He says, and then trust in that Word so much that you are willing to do exactly what He says. Do you really believe that Psalms 139:16 is true? Do you believe "that all the days ordained for [you] were written in [His] book before one of them came to be?"

Do you honestly believe that God has a specific plan for your life? Are you certain that you (with His help) can fulfill that plan?

If your answers were "no" or "maybe," you need to ask yourself why. Is it because you don't believe Him or because you don't believe in yourself? Let me assure you that God never lies, and He already said He has plans for you. Let me also assure you that it isn't about what you can do; it isn't about your strengths or your weaknesses. It's about what He can do through you. So don't get so caught up in your failures that you don't allow Him to move you on to victories.

If your answers were "yes," then you are ready to hear from Him. Although His vision is not some "thing" that He will tell you in one word, He does often show you the next step in your chapter. Sometimes He might even give you a little excerpt from a chapter that is still to come. It just depends on Him, and His timing is always right. So make it a priority to seek to know His plans for your life on a consistent basis. If you have a major decision to make about your future, seek Him for direction! That means more than a "God, help me make the right decision" prayer before you mail in that college application. That means you spend as much time as it takes waiting for His guidance. It could be a direct word from Him, a feeling of peace, or a sense of uneasiness about the choice that you are making. He speaks in many ways, but you must seek to hear Him first!

Still, even after seeking His direction, at times in my life I felt like I was driving in fog. Although I knew the general direction I was headed, I could see only a couple feet ahead of me. I earnestly prayed for God to lift the fog a little, to give me a glimpse of what was ten feet ahead. You know what? Sometimes He did give me that glimpse, but usually He just encouraged me to keep walking. Though I would have preferred to see the entire landscape, God taught me so much more about faith by allowing me to only see a couple feet at a time. Driving in fog is not the most enjoyable way to travel down the road, and it's definitely not the most time efficient. But sometimes the fastest and easiest way to get to your destination won't teach you anything but how to save time. God's method of travel always takes you someplace you've never seen before, and the lessons learned are worth the extra time.

> "Since, then, you have been raised with Christ, set your hearts on things above, where Christ is seated at the right hand of God. Set your minds on things above, not on earthly things." (Colossians 3:1-2)

In order to live out God's vision for your life, you must seek to hear from Him first. Instead, some of you first seek to hear from your guidance counselor, your best friend, your favorite teacher, your boyfriend, or your parents. Even though it is often good to seek their advice, they cannot take the place of seeking to hear from Him. He's the only one who knows what is written in the next chapter of your book. He's the only one who knows the vision He has for your life.

So how do you figure out what God's purpose is for your life? How do you discover who you are meant to be? You live your life sincerely believing that God really does have a specific plan for your life, that He really does have an amazing vision for you, a book of all that your life could and should be. You live your life seeking to know that plan, and you stay in contact with the author. You make it a priority to spend time with Him so that you can hear His voice, so that you can point your skis in the right direction. Then, you live His plan, walking each day in submission to Him. **You strive to wake up each morning saying, "More of You, and less of me."** You come to the place where you can honestly say, **"God, whatever You ask, whenever You ask it, I will do it."**

Proverbs 29:18 states,

"Where there is no vision, the people perish."

People without direction and purpose do little with their life and lead a miserable existence. The good news is that none of you are without vision. God has already prepared a detailed blueprint for your life, but you choose how you will actually build the life that you have been given. Will you seek to know the chapters in His book for you, or will you try to write your own?

If you plan to live your life according to Jeremiah 29:11, you won't get to the end of your life and realize that you forgot to truly live. You won't wake up one day and regret that you led an unproductive and unfulfilled life. You won't wander around aimlessly through life, continually in search of your purpose. What you will do at the end of your life is discover that you walked through each chapter in your book—the incredible vision that He wrote especially for you. You will discover that you became the exact woman that God meant for you to be. You will see that you lived a life worth living. You will figure out that 1 Corinthians 2:9 is actually true:

"... No eye has seen, no ear has heard, no mind has conceived what God has prepared for those who love Him."

You, even with all the wisdom of your human mind, cannot begin to imagine the crazy awesome things God has planned for you. All you have to do is give Him your entire life—your time, your hurts, your dreams, your priorities, your everything. He'll take care of the rest. So don't miss out on His offer. Start now, and never look back. You choose today what your tomorrow with be.

By the way, if you would like to keep wearing His glasses so that you can more clearly see who you are, who He is, who Christians really are, and who you are created to be, that's more than okay. You don't have to return them. Actually, God has always had a pair reserved just for you. He's always wanted you to see life through His eyes because, put simply, what He sees is truth. So continue to wear His glasses until you no longer notice that they are there. Wear them until they are simply a part of you. You won't regret it.

2 Peter 1:3

"His divine power has given us everything we need for life and godliness through our knowledge of Him who called us by His own glory and goodness."

Reflection Questions

1. How can spills affect God's blueprint of your life?

2. What are the "spills" that you are dealing with right now?

3. What excuses have you used to explain why you can't fulfill God's vision for your life?

4. How do you feel about this statement: "Show me your friends, and I'll show you your future"?

5. Make a list of your friends. Do you have a Moses? Are you being a Moses to someone? Who is impacting you?

6. Why do we experience hard times?

7. What's the hardest thing you've had to deal with so far in life? How did you get through? What did God do for you?

8. Are you ready to live out God's vision for your life, or does the thought of living your life that way overwhelm you? Why do we sometimes feel overwhelmed by living our lives as we're created to live them?

1. Wikipedia, s.v. "eating disorders." http://en.wikipedia.org/wiki/Eating_disorder.

2. See <http://kidshealth.org/teen/food_fitness/problems/eat_disorder.html>.

3. See <http://www.finestquotes.com/author_quotes-author-Edward%20Conklin-page-0.htm>.

4. "Never Alone" copyright 2004 by Barlow Girl. From the CD *Barlow Girl* copyright 2004 Fervent Records.

5. See <http://en.wikiquote.org/wiki/C._S._Lewis>.

6. Barna Group, "A New Generation Expresses its Skepticism and Frustration with Christianity," September 24, 2007, www.barna.org/barna-update/article/16-teensnext-gen/94-a-new-generation-expresses-its-skepticism-and-frustration-with-christianity.

7. Barna Group, "A New Generation Expresses its Skepticism and Frustration with Christianity," September 24, 2007, www.barna.org/barna-update/article/16-teensnext-gen/94-a-new-generation-expresses-its-skepticism-and-frustration-with-christianity.

8. See <http://christianquotes.org/tag/cat/72>.

9. Wayne Cordeiro, *The Divine Mentor* (Bloomington, MN: Bethany House Publishing, 2007), 102.

10. See <http://en.wikiquote.org/wiki/C._S._Lewis>.

11. Webster's New World Dictionary, Third College Edition (New York, NY: Simon and Schuster, 1988), s.v. "humility."

12. Webster's New World Dictionary, Third College Edition (New York, NY: Simon and Schuster, 1988), s.v. "pride."

13. "Give Me Your Eyes" copyright 2008 by Brandon Heath. From the CD *What If We* copyright 2008 Reunion Records.

14. Anne Lammott as quoted in Mark Batterson, *Wild Goose Chase* (Colorado Springs, CO: Multnomah Books, 2008), 163.

15. Webster's New World Dictionary, Third College Edition (New York, NY: Simon and Schuster, 1988), s.v. "freedom."

16. Corrie Ten Boom, *The Hiding Place* (Washington Depot, Connecticut: Chosen Books, 1971), 190.

17. Mark Batterson, *Wild Goose Chase* (Colorado Springs, CO: Multnomah Books 2008), 79.

18. See <http://www.famousquotesandauthors.com/authors/corrie_ten_boom_quotes.html>.

19. See <http://thinkexist.com/quotation/to_one_who_has_faith-no_explanation_is_necessary/149677.html>.

Appendix: Small Group Materials

A Note to Small Group Leaders

First, let me just start out by saying, "Congratulations!" You have volunteered for the best job in the world—working with young ladies. You get the incredible opportunity of guiding them through a time in their lives when they are most moldable. How cool is that? But with that job also comes responsibility. You will become both their role model and their example of how a Christian woman should live. So I challenge you to be able to look into your girls' eyes and honestly say what Paul did in I Cor. 11:1: "Follow my example as I follow the example of Christ." Lead the way in your desire and passion for Him. Be sure to fulfill all of the same expectations that you have for your girls—the scripture memorization included!

I've included a variety of extra materials in this section designed to help you use this book to lead your small groups. "A Note to His Girls" explains the basic idea of the book and asks those in small groups to make a commitment to meeting its expectations. Walk them through this commitment, and help them understand that this small group study is written specifically for girls who have a desire to grow in their knowledge of and relationship with God. You may likely have some girls who are not ready for the challenge, and they will, unfortunately, begin to show up less often. Although it will break your heart, and you will want to force them to make a commitment, let them go. You can't force desire, but you can pray that they will begin to be dissatisfied with where they are in their journey with Him.

Following each chapter of this book are questions you may discuss together as a group and a scripture to memorize for your next group time. The idea is that the girls will come having read the chapter you assigned, answered the discussion questions, and memorized the verse, which can be written on their "Weekly Update." (Feel free to make copies of both the "Weekly Update" and "Taking it to God.")

In addition, you will find a "Basic Outline for a Small Group" (page 192) that gives you a detailed breakdown of how you can organize your time together. I've also given you some additional, "Extra Ideas for Group Times" (page 194) that offer activities for each chapter, beyond just discussing the questions. Depending on the age of your students, you may feel that you need to word some of the questions slightly differently, or alter the activity in a way that will work better for your group. Each group is slightly different from one another, and you know what will best help the girls in your group grow in their spiritual understanding and relationship with Christ!

Discussion is obviously a big part of what you will do during your time together, but realize that it is a process. Don't become discouraged if you seem to be doing most of the talking in the beginning. It may be a little rough at first, especially if your girls are less talkative or don't know each other very well, but don't worry. As they learn to trust each other and trust you, your discussion times will become easier (and longer, too!) Make sure and stress the confidentiality of the group. What is said in group stays in group.

I also want to challenge you to pray on a consistent basis for the girls in your small group. Pray for their needs, but also pray the following scripture over their lives. (Insert the names of your girls in the blanks.)

> "I KEEP ASKING THAT THE GOD OF OUR LORD JESUS CHRIST, THE GLORIOUS FATHER, MAY GIVE ________ THE SPIRIT OF WISDOM AND REVELATION, SO THAT ____________ MAY KNOW HIM BETTER. I PRAY ALSO THAT THE EYES OF ____________'S HEART MAY BE ENLIGHTENED IN ORDER THAT ________ MAY KNOW THE HOPE TO WHICH HE HAS CALLED ________, THE RICHES OF HIS GLORIOUS INHERITANCE IN THE SAINTS, AND HIS INCOMPARABLY GREAT POWER FOR US WHO BELIEVE." (EPHESIANS 1:17-19)

Thanks so much for giving of your time and energy for these young ladies. You are making an impact on generations to come, though you will likely never know the full extent of that impact. You are awesome. Have a great time discovering together how to see life through a different pair of glasses!

Basic Outline for a Small Group

- Have the girls fill out their "Weekly Update." Collect them, praise those who have memorized the verse, and take note of the ones who are willing to share something from the last week. (I've found that candy is a great incentive for scripture memorization.) While they are filling these out, return the "Weekly Update" from last week. Before returning these sheets, I usually both read and write comments on them as a way of encouraging and/or challenging the girls in their relationship with Him. (I would strongly encourage you to provide folders or binders for the girls, so that they can keep all of their small group materials together.)

- Share about what God has been up to. This is the time to ask those willing students to share what God has been doing in their lives. Make sure that you are ready to share something too. It is vital for the girls to hear what God is doing in your life as well, and it reinforces the importance of journaling!

- Jump into an overview of the part of the chapter that was read for this week. You (or a student) could do a quick summary of the main points. (This helps if someone is new and serves as a reminder of what they've already read.)

- Begin discussing the questions and/or doing any other activity that goes along with their reading. (See "Extra

Ideas for Group Times" on page 194.) Try to keep the discussion moving and on track!

- Make sure the students understand what is required of them for next time. They are to read the next part of the chapter, memorize the scripture, and answer the discussion questions prior to coming to the next small group.

- Do prayer requests/answers to prayer. I've found this to be a vital part of knowing what is going on in the lives of the girls. Though at times, I do have to cut this short, or ask that the girls keep it to a maximum of 2 or 3 so that everyone can share, I try to do this every small group time. You can do prayer a number of different ways. You could ask the girls to pray for the one of the right or the left out loud or quietly. You may just ask for volunteers to pray aloud for certain requests or over all the requests. Or you can divide the girls into groups of 2 or 3 to pray for each other. Make sure to impress upon them the importance of writing down each others' requests and praying for them throughout the week. (This is the time to use the "Taking it to God" sheet.)

- Do something just for fun and fellowship. Sometimes this is simply eating and talking. Other times it might be an actual game or activity. Whatever it is, it's a great time for connecting with the girls and for them to connect with each other.

Extra Ideas for Group Times

Each chapter is followed by questions for the girls to come ready to share and discuss during the group times. The following are additional ideas that may also be used.

Chapter 1

Play a fun get-to-know one another game. Give each girl a blank piece of paper and instruct them all to write something about themselves that no one else in the group knows. Have them turn in the papers without their names on them. Then, read the papers aloud to the girls. The group tries to guess who wrote the description. You can learn a lot of interesting facts about each other in this game, and it forces the girls to begin thinking about who they are.

Chapter 2

Have each girl write her name in the middle of a blank piece of paper and put it on the floor or a table. (Or, if you want to get more creative, bring scrapbooking materials, markers, stickers, etc., and have the girls make a page with their name on it.) Each person in the group must then write a strength or a God-given gift that she sees in each girl in the group. When every girl has written on everyone else's sheet, ask them to find their papers and read them aloud to the group. Then, encourage the girls to hang those sheets in a prominent place in their room to serve as a reminder of all the strengths that God has blessed them with. (If they are using small group folders/binders to hold their prayer request sheets, journaling pages, and accountability sheets, you could also do this activity on the back of that folder, or have the girls keep the sheet in their folders.)

Chapter 3

Have the girls find a place to get alone with God to read over Psalms 139 about how great God's love is for them. Then they are to honestly answer whether they believe that they are that crystal goblet instead of the Styrofoam cup. Leaders can go around to each girl asking for her answer and praying with each individually.

Another idea: Get a Styrofoam cup and a crystal goblet and compare them. Then, hold up a Styrofoam cup, making the point that some girls wrongly see themselves as it instead of the goblet. Poke holes in the Styrofoam (symbolizing what happens when girls believe others' negative words). Then, pour water into the cup (symbolizing God's love running out because the girls cannot accept that He loves them). Pour water into the goblet, and make the point that holes cannot be punched in it. Girls that see themselves as goblets can accept God's love because they see themselves as they really are.

Chapter 4

Go to a craft store, and buy each girl a small mirror and some decorating stuff—ribbons, glue, paint, markers, stickers, foam, glitter, etc. Use foam to frame the mirrors, and then be creative with the decorating! Make sure to write some scripture references about true beauty on them! (I Peter 3:3-4, Proverbs 31:30)

Another idea: Watch a Dove Ad called "Evolution" on youtube.com and discuss it. (I would highly recommend this video!)

Chapter 5

Let the girls know that you are going to do a very serious role play that they may or may not have already encountered in real life. Then, tell them that you are one of their best friends at school, and they have just noticed marks on your arms that suggest you've been cutting. Have each of the girls act out what she would do or say. Impress the seriousness of the situation and the importance of knowing how to react to their friends.

Chapter 6

As an introductory question, ask the girls how they know that wind is real. You will likely hear some things about seeing trees move, etc. Make the point that we can't actually see wind, but we can see its effects. Just because we can't see something, does it mean it's not there? Compare this with the reality of God.
Another idea: Play the song "Never Alone" by Barlow Girl and discuss the lyrics. Have they ever felt the way the songwriter felt?

Chapter 7

Set up a mock tabernacle and use Lev. 16 to go through the process that a high priest had to go through to go into the Most Holy Place. Have one of the girls (who has a dramatic flair) act out the part of the high priest. You could make this real simple and use a sheet for the curtain, an end table for the altar, stuffed animal for the sacrifice, bath robe for the priestly garments. The goal is for the girls to understand how blessed they are to now have free access to God—that the curtain is now torn in two.

Chapter 8

Have the girls dig through their purses/bags and make a pile of all the things that their parents provide for them. Examples: money, cell phone, clothes, food, car (keys), etc. Then make a pile of all the things their heavenly Dad has provided for them. (They could write these on pieces of paper.) Compare the two piles and discuss.

Chapter 9

Set up an obstacle course. You could use chairs, tables, whatever you have. Have one girl blindfold herself, and then ask two girls to give her advice on how to get through the course. One of the girls is to give her good advice, and the other is to give her wrong advice. The girl who is blindfolded has to decide who she will listen to. Make the point that Jesus always gives us good advice, even when we can't really see where we are going. He always knows the way.

Chapter 10

Ask for a volunteer to lie down on the floor on a large piece of paper. (A roll of paper works best, but you could use the back of wrapping paper or a couple of poster boards taped together.) Have the others draw an outline of the student's body on the paper. Then ask the whole group to sit around the outline. Ask them these questions: What are the 1st things that come to mind when you hear the word "Christian"? What are the 1st things that might come to some of your unsaved friends' minds when they hear the word "Christian"? Discuss their thoughts. Write the ones that are right descriptions of a Christian on the inside of the outline. Write the ones that are misperceptions on the outside of the outline.

Another idea: Draw two outlines instead of just one. After drawing the outlines, tell the girls that the first outline represents a Christian, and the second represents a non-Christian. Have them write their descriptions of each inside the designated outlines. Compare their descriptions and discuss.

Chapter 11

Discuss the chapter while sitting around an actual campfire and eating s'mores! What a great visual of what you're discussing! If weather doesn't permit, you could always move the party inside around a fireplace. Or, if that's not possible either, you could always use candles and replace the toasted marshmallows with marshmallow creme!

Chapter 12

Have the girls write down an hour-by-hour description of everything they did either yesterday or today (whichever they can remember the best). Make the point that life will always be busy, and schedules will normally be full, but it is up to them to determine what they will do with the time they have. Discuss how most of their time is spent, and how much time they gave to spending time with God.

Chapter 13

Place a trashcan in the middle of the group. Then, ask the girls to write down on a sheet of paper some ways that they have hurt God in the past. Be sure to reassure them that if they have sincerely asked forgiveness for those things, He has forgiven them, and that He loves them. Then, have them tear up those papers and throw them into the trash can to illustrate His forgiveness and love. Next, ask the students to write down some ways that people have hurt them in the past. Make the point that even though these people may not deserve their forgiveness, we didn't deserve God's forgiveness either. Christ calls us to love our enemies and to pray for those who have wronged us. Have them pray about whether they have forgiven the people who have hurt them. As they feel like they are ready, instruct them to tear up the paper and throw it away, symbolizing their willingness to forgive and even learn to love those people. (You could also do this outside and throw the papers into a fire.)
Another idea: Play Brandon Heath's song "Give Me Your Eyes" and discuss it.

Chapter 14

Teach the girls how to fight! Ask one of the girls to volunteer, and then dress her for battle. Use Ephesians 6:10-18, and actually have the props to go with it (belt, breastplate, shoes, shield, helmet, sword). You might have to improvise a little! Discuss what each one does and why it's important.

Chapter 15

Ask each of the girls to write down one example of a situation that she has gone through that was a "tough time" and how she reacted to it. Help them decide if they chose to react correctly in those situations or not. Did they choose joy? Did they choose to think on the things mentioned in Phil. 4:8 instead of the focusing on negative thoughts? Did they learn anything from that situation?

Chapter 16

Get a piece of wood and glue two different action figures on it—one on each end. Raise the hands of one of them—symbolizing living dangerously for God. The other figure represents "just doing enough to get by" in their walk with God. Put the wood in a place where the rest of the group cannot see it. Then, instruct each girl to use a colored marker and place a mark on the wood to symbolize where she is currently living. Then, have the girls use a different colored marker to symbolize where they want to be. After each girl has made her marks, tell her to find a place to pray about how she can be where she wants to be.

Chapter 17

Use construction paper to make book covers for God's book for their lives. The girls can decorate the outside by drawing (or cutting out from magazines or photos) the things that are most important to them. Inside the cover, have them write down things that God has used them to do in the past, things He is using them to do now, and some ways they think

God might use them in the future. Discuss how His vision for their lives is everything their lives could be and should be now, tomorrow, and 10 years from now.

Chapter 18

Find a rather thick book that you don't mind throwing away. (A phonebook would work.) That book symbolizes God's vision for their life. Then, put the book in some sort of basin, open it up, and pour a little colored liquid (like Kool-Aid) over it. Show the girls how the spill will affect many pages of the book, not just one or two. Continue to pour the liquid over the pages of the book as you discuss how it symbolizes what can happen in their lives. Show them how having a spill in the front of the book will affect how the middle of it looks. Make the point that spills will affect their future.

Your name:

IN THE PAST WEEK . . .

Where in the Bible have you been reading?

Would you be willing to share something God did in your life this week? (You could share a scripture you read that stood out, an answer to a prayer, an opportunity you had to share Him with someone, an entry from your spiritual journal, how youth service impacted you, etc.)

What/who have you been praying for?

Check one that best describes your feelings:

___ I feel good about my time with God this week.

___ I wish I would have spent more time with God this week.

If you checked the second one, why do you feel this way? What kept you from spending the time you wanted to spend with Him?

Write the scripture you memorized for this week.

Taking it to God

Date	Name of person requesting prayer	Description of the Need	How was the need answered? (yes, no, maybe...)

A Note to His Girls

You are about to embark on a journey that is designed to help you grow in your knowledge and understanding of your Creator. It is written specifically for a girl who has already given her life to God, has a desire to know Him more, and is willing to do whatever it takes to become the woman she is created to be. Because discovering your full potential is of utmost importance, some things will be expected of you throughout the course of this journey. You will be expected to be at your group times regularly, to read each chapter and answer the questions that follow, to memorize scriptures, and to spend personal time with God on a consistent basis. These expectations are not meant to be a burden to you. They are meant to help you realize, understand, and live God's vision for your life. If you are ready to embark on this journey together, please sign your name below stating your commitment to your decision. Then, hold on tight for a wild adventure of discovering who you are, who He is, who His followers are, and who you were created to be. By the way, at the end of this journey, you may find yourself wearing a pair of glasses that you didn't even realize you owned . . .

I will try my very best to meet the expectations of this small group. I want to live a life that allows Him to continually stretch my potential.

____

Signature Date

Search for the Truth Publications

Mail-In Order Form

E-MAIL, SEND, OR CALL:

SEARCH FOR THE TRUTH MINISTRIES
TRUTH@SEARCHFORTHETRUTH.NET
3275 MONROE RD.
MIDLAND, MI 48642
989.837.5546

	Price per book			
	Single	**2-9**	**10+**	**Case Price**
Borrowing God's Glasses	11.95	8.95	6.00	Call
A Closer Look at the Evidence	11.95	8.95	6.00	Call
Protecting God's Workmanship	11.95	8.95	6.00	Call
Censored Science	14.95	11.95	7.50	Call

Resource	**Quan.**	**Cost Each**	**Total**
Borrowing God's Glasses			
A Closer Look at the Evidence			
Censored Science			
Protecting God's Workmanship			
		Subtotal	
		MI residents add 6% sales tax	
		Shipping : add 15% of subtotal	
		TOTAL ENCLOSED	

Ship Order To

NAME:

ADDRESS:

CITY/ST/ZIP:

PHONE:

- Please make checks payable to "Search for the Truth Ministries"
- Normal delivery time is 1-2 weeks
- For express delivery, increase shipping to 20% of order

Other Resources

A Closer Look at the Evidence is another one-of-a-kind book from Search for the Truth Publications. Organized in 26 different scientific areas, each page ties together God's Word with God's world. Great for use as a daily devotional! Softcover, 414 pg, $5^{1/2}$ x $8^{1/2}$

Censored Science: The Suppressed Evidence is the most graphically stunning book we have ever offered. Every page is both a visual masterpiece in full color and intellectually mind opening. Learn what is being left out of student textbooks. Written in an understandable and fascinating way! Softcover, 112 pg, $8^{1/2}$ x 11

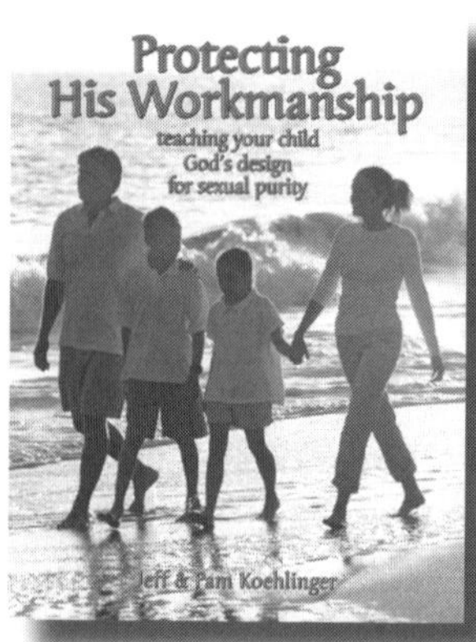

Protecting His Workmanship provides help for the parent child "sex-talk". This interactive and thoroughly biblical study is a wonderful resource for equipping teens to stay sexually pure in our sex-saturated society. Softcover workbook, 112 pg, $8^{1/2}$ x 11

SEE ALL OUR RESOURCES AT WWW.SEARCHFORTHETRUTH.NET

SHARE THE GLASSES!

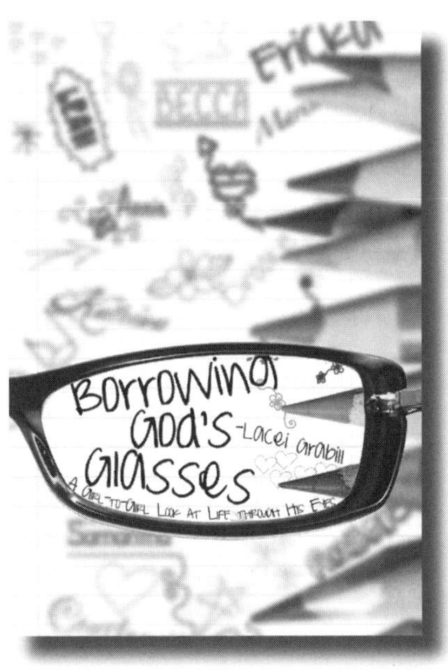

Do you lead a small group?
Does your church have ministry specifically for teenagers?

Borrowing God's Glasses is a perfect book to prepare youth for the "real life" that is racing towards them. Written by a mother of three who has spent the majority of her adult life working with teens, this book hits home with adolescent girls. Filled with scripture and real-life stories, it has the right stuff to transform a teen's life. But it can't do any of this sitting on the shelf. Give it as a gift, introduce a copy to your youth leaders, or see if your church can provide one for the entire youth group. (Softcover, 208pg, $5^{1/2}$ x $8^{1/2}$)

Multiple copies as low as $5.00 each!